MOLE RANCH

Life in our Log Cabin in the

Mountains of North Carolina

J. Privette

For all of our mountain friends

who welcomed us, helped us and

made our time at the cabin

the richly memorable experience that it was

INTRODUCTION

Imagine a night with no moon. Deep in a mountain cove, surrounded by the shapeless dark forest, the only lights are stars sprayed over a narrow black canopy, silent except for the sigh of wind rolling down the ridge, the whisper of leaves restless under starlight.

Nights at our cabin in the mountains were that sort of profound peace for our family. The lightless pasture with boxwoods and old black walnut trees casting dull shadows from the cabin glow. The limits of constellations defining the ridgetops above the cove, a barred owl hooting lowly in the near distance. We knew the rabbits huddled in their dens while we read by the fire, happy to be one whole family together in our home.

We did not know what life we would uncover when we moved to our log cabin in the mountains, but we welcomed the change from our urban life. It was to be a simpler life filled with new experiences and new understanding, but in the beginning we knew only that it felt right.

WHY MOVE?

My wife, Beth, and I spent a decade in Atlanta. Before moving to the cabin, our children had never lived anywhere other than Atlanta. Both were born in Northside Hospital in Atlanta. Both began school at St. Martin in the Fields School in Atlanta. All of their friends lived in Atlanta. Our family has many good memories. All in all, Atlanta had been fun; nevertheless, it became time for us to move.

When we decided to move from Atlanta to the mountains of North Carolina outside of Asheville, it was not because we had become disenchanted with life in a sprawling metropolis. We were not pursuing a dream of a better quality of life or getting back to nature or rediscovering our agrarian roots. We were not even fleeing the congestion and bad air of a commuter lifestyle, though we should have.

The simple reason for our move was that we are natives of North Carolina and always felt that we were temporary residents of Atlanta. We had moved from Raleigh, North Carolina to Atlanta in 1991. Beth and I grew up in small eastern North Carolina towns and had no ambition to live in a city larger than Raleigh, which was then more of a big town than a small city despite the local boosterism. But the company I worked for invited me to make the change, and we thought it might be exciting to live in Atlanta for a few years. After nearly ten years passed, we began to think it was not all that exciting any more. We missed our home state and being closer to family.

During the decade of the 1990s, the Atlanta metro area population grew over one million people. Home prices doubled inside the Perimeter and average commute times stretched beyond a half hour each way, leading the nation and surpassing even Los Angeles, the ultimate commuter culture. We had friends who could get to work in an hour *if* they left home by 6 AM; for them, getting home was another challenge, taking as much as two hours on rainy evenings. It could take fifteen minutes to drive Peachtree Street the few blocks from north of Phipps Plaza to south of Lenox Square mall in the middle of the day. Beth began to spend most of her day in the car as she carpooled the children to school, ran errands, picked up children from school and took them to soccer or a friends' home, then picked them up again to try to be home in time for a late dinner. Fatigue became permanent.

But that was the day-to-day grind. Most of the time we lived there, we enjoyed what Atlanta had to offer. Lots of great restaurants. A good art museum and zoo. Plays, the summer film series at the Fox Theater, ballet (Baryshnikov and Twyla Tharp performing together), outdoor concerts at Chastain Park (which the City is in the process of trying to strangle into silence;

it seems that a lot of the new residents who moved to the nicely located Chastain Park area like the idea of a park, but have decided that they do not want to hear the music any longer), the symphony (with and without James Taylor), Cirque du Soleil, bicycle races (with Lance Armstrong before he was famous or infamous), and, of course, the 1996 Summer Olympics.

Despite the fun, we always wanted to return to North Carolina. Our families still lived in North Carolina, and we wanted to be where we could visit more easily than the eight to ten hour drive from Atlanta up Interstate 85. Mostly, we never thought of ourselves as Atlantans even though we had lived there longer than many of the people we knew.

We began to look at property in our old home state. North of Greensboro, east of Edenton. We looked for a hook, a reason to select one part of the state over another. We knew the eastern part of the state well though not the northeast. Beans Weatherly of Elizabeth City showed us around the Albemarle country and made us feel most welcome. Historic preservationists in Eden did the same in the foothill country between Greensboro and Virginia. The countryside north of the Triad was still remote enough to have a farm and drive to Greensboro for a nice dinner. We fell in love with properties in both areas but could not make all the pieces fit together.

Then, my best friend, Todd, convinced me that I needed to visit him in Asheville.

Beth had taught school in Asheville when she graduated from college. I had been to Asheville a few times, but only to visit Biltmore Estate. I had passed through several times on my way to hike the western mountains in Slickrock Wilderness or the Great Smoky Mountains. Asheville had been less than a blur on a fast interstate passage. I had no idea what the town was like.

Todd convinced me that downtown was interesting, that old buildings were being renovated and converted from commercial, office or warehouse to residential. He kept an apartment in the old Asheville

Hotel on Haywood Street. Downstairs was Malaprops, one of the best independent booksellers in the country. Malaprops sponsors readings by talent both fresh and durable with a decided bias for native North Carolina writers and women authors, neither of which you will find in a national chain bookstore with any reliability or regularity.

When I finally visited, I found good restaurants; Flying Frog was for years one of our favorites, serving an eclectic menu of daily specials that I would not do justice in describing as East Indian Fusion, but whose duck was unsurpassed with a wine list to boot. Formal Italian at Vincenzo's on brick-paved Market Street and casual café Italian at La Catarina on Pack Square (unfortunately, since relocated outside of downtown). Tupelo Honey served nouveau Southern breakfast fare until four in the morning. Limones, Table, Wasabi, Beanstreets, Gold Hill Coffee, Mediterranean Café, Bistro 1848, Noodle House, Salsa's. You get the idea. A cornucopia of cuisines and not a chain restaurant in sight.

A good and burgeoning selection of bars and brew pubs. The basics serve a proper selection of fine ales as well as the excellent local brews: Highland and French Broad. Jack of the Wood is a true pub in the best Irish or British tradition with a live Celtic ceilidh on Sunday nights and serving its own Green Man Ales. Most surprising of all is Zambra's, a tapas bar under the old Asheville Hotel, specializing in Spanish wines and exotic imported ales (not a Budweiser in the house).

The downtown Fine Arts Theatre (sponsoring movies that are artistically excellent, but do not meet the Hollywood test of financially stunning results). Diana Wortham Theater, Asheville Community Theatre, 35 Below, North Carolina Stage Company and other intimate performance venues. The Orange Peel, a renovated 1950s African-American night club with nightly bands. Pack Place with a small art museum and an interactive children's experience called Health Adventures. The renovated Grove Arcade, an indoor promenade framed by marble and ornate architecture, one the country's earliest malls.

Downtown Asheville, though small, offered everything that modern American cities hope to offer. Walkable streets with a healthy mixture of cultures and cuisines.

In short, Asheville is urbane, but with the soul of a small mountain town. A miniature Paris with Appalachian flavor. What drew the wealthy northerners (we call them "Yankees" still) at the turn of the twentieth century continues to attract people.

By day, we enjoyed much that the mountains offer. Cool air, cold streams, hiking, biking, horseback riding. By night, we strolled the downtown streets and relaxed with locally brewed ale listening to bluegrass. Or toured the arts and crafts galleries.

Outside of downtown Asheville, the mountains were still populated with self-sufficient people. People willing to lend a hand or a solution. People who loved, as we did, open space, lush pastures with horses and cattle grazing peacefully alongside lively creeks and winding roads.

One such person was Harlan Sawyer. Harlan lived with his wife and sons on an eleven acre farm near Warren Wilson College, almost due north of our cabin over the mountain. I bought prime firewood from Harlan. It was prime because he cared about selling the best firewood he could find and because he was hard-working and proud of his work, his family and their farm.

Harlan dropped off two cords of wood early in our second autumn. He cut the wood when he was not working for the postal service. His wife was a teacher. Harlan brought the firewood stacked neat as library books on his two-ton flatbed truck. He usually dropped off the wood about eight in the evening. And he always had time to chat a while. We had long, rambling discussions about our families, the world, the economy and, naturally, firewood. I cannot recall how we stitched all those topics together, but our conversation flowed easily from one to the other, as if we had been friends for life and had a lifetime to share our thoughts. On that particular night, we covered the following:

- Blueberries for fun or profit
- Tomatoes. How local farmers are shipping theirs to California and we could not find any fresh home-grown locally.
- The price of diesel fuel and whether gas prices would drop below $3.00 per gallon in the wake of Hurricane Katrina and the devastation to the Gulf.
- Retirement. He and "the wife" hoped to retire in about four years. Harlan would be 56.
- Mastitis in dairy cows (his).
- Farming for a living. His son would like to, but Harlan did not think that was realistic.
- Paying for college for our children.
- Salvaging cut timber from the new phase of a prominent local subdivision where the cutting of a new road

apparently disturbed a rattlesnake den, scattering small (but poisonous) small rattlers throughout the neighborhood.

- The end of an unusually warm and humid summer.
- Our families.

Harlan never got out of his truck. In all the years that I knew him, he never did. Ours was the kind of restful chat that, like leaning over your neighbor's fence, you cannot have too often. It connected me with the real world in a way none of my business conversations ever could.

We cherished being able to enjoy what a city such as Asheville offered while also being able to live away from the city on land where we could heard the leaves of our poplar trees rustle with the breeze and the murmuring chatter of our creek tumbling over rocks -- a place where we not only could hear the wind and the creek, but where it was quiet enough to *notice* that we heard them.

Growth in places as beautiful as those mountains was inevitable. The mountains as we knew them would change. Some changes would seem for the better, like the widening of Old Charlotte Highway (Drovers' Road) from a curvy two-lane scenic by-way to a sleek, five-lane highway. Now traffic flows even during the busy autumn leaf season.

However, improvement, like beauty, is in the eye of the beholder. I enjoyed the convenience of being able to streak into town, but preferred the former charm of the lazy mountain road the same way I continued to enjoy a drive over Hickory Nut Gap into the Gorge and down through Bat Cave to Lake Lure. Convenience comes at a price.

The new highway brought convenience to all and prosperity to some. It was easier to get to work, and landowners along the highway will one day reap the windfall of rising land values. The initial cost of this convenience was the loss of a charming mountain road.

The ongoing cost may be the loss of rural character that is endemic to small and winding roads. I preferred the hustle and bustle of that same road through Bat Cave, where the road was too narrow (not widened yet), the traffic too crowded, and cars, bikers and pedestrians all mixed in a festival atmosphere.

What I truly loved was what I imagined were remnants of what the countryside had been twenty years previous. I imagined an agrarian economy that was mostly sustenance, a farmer raising crops and livestock to feed his family and his livestock. His perennial hope would have been to have more than he needed after enjoying fresh vegetables all summer and sharing or trading them with neighbors. He hoped to have enough left to can and preserve for the winter and spring until the following summer's crop would be ripe for harvest. He hoped, maybe, there might even be enough to sell for a bit of cash.

I imagined a community of people who shared the joys and disappointments of a life that could be hard and unforgiving in the way that nature always is. They did the best they could with what nature yielded or withheld, and their neighbors did the same. Faith was a force that bound them as much as shared plight or destiny. A late spring frost kills young plants regardless the farmer, his politics or his wealth. The people of the mountain community were both independent and interdependent. All were willing to lend a hand to others in need.

There was a good man, Tom, who lived at the bottom of our cove and raised beef cattle. His roots extended three generations back in our cove, back to a time when the only people who lived up the cove were the Wright family, the pioneers who built our cabin. He pieced together his 80 acre farm to restore some of the family's original twelve hundred acre land holdings. He knew the value of his land as it was – bottomland pasture stretching along Cane Creek.

He declared to me one afternoon, "It'll stay this way so long as I'm alive."

We need more like Tom, people who see the value of preserving what they have, not selling just because they can sell for money, slowing the pace of change so that the mountains might continue to be for as long as possible what many of us have loved about the primitive and undeveloped.

THE CABIN

"It's so cute and authentic," a passing cyclist once described our cabin to her companion, speaking as if I was not standing in the pasture near the creek and road, hearing her every word as clearly as if she spoke to me. But she was quite right; the cabin was that and more. Charming and warm. Old. Mid-19th century. A veritable antique.

The cabin, the entire homestead, was a found poem. It was what it was and not what we might have made it had we made it. Lacking the perfection of being our personal design – not that we would have made it perfect, but only that it might have been perfect in that it would have been our design – it was perfect in being what it was. A goal for my own life, accepting truth as it is and not as I wish it to be.

The beauty lay in what we discovered it to be and to have been, not what we might have made of it. The exquisite nature of its perfection was that it was what it was including all of its flaws and errors and imperfections. All of which was in addition to that which was, in fact, perfect. Form following function in its elegant simplicity. Being so of the earth and the mountains and the land and the woods. Having been constructed in and of this place. The logs fitting together into walls and representing the joinery of the elements of this homestead, the trees – chestnut, oak, white pine – and the stones, rocks worn smooth by timeless flow of the creek.

Years of neglect left the land rough, the natural beauty of untended grounds, unshaped and ancient boxwoods marking the perimeter of the yard just behind a low stone wall. The tangible connection to time and change in the insect-ravaged south wall. The worn and weathered wood of siding silver and gray with grain traced like a carving in time.

Tucked in the dark and unvisited corners of the garage, shed and barn, small collections of fiber, leaf, straw, bark and grass. Nests. Mouse, squirrel, swallow. Like the cabin, the nests were a testament to form with function, an elemental grace at once simple and irrepeatably complex. Unique design that cannot be duplicated except through intent.

When I first saw the cabin, I looked past any of its flaws. I saw only what it should be and could be, how I would feel living in it and how I thought our family would feel being a family in it. I was not wrong. I was very right, even if underestimating the effect it would have on all of us.

It is a log cabin made of hand-hewn logs, made by the hands of the settlers who adopted this land and committed to survive in a dark, lonely and remote cove with barely a path width between ridge and creek. The logs were shaped with rough and essential tools – an ax and adze. The sides of the logs are flat, having been shaved and squared by the adze. The log sides show the chops and cuts of the adze, the pattern of parallel slices into the wood revealing the nature of human shaping. The tops and bottoms of the logs retain the curve of the tree trunk, bark stripped and limbs trimmed, but otherwise unformed by human hands. Chinking fills the uneven spaces between the logs, concrete troweled over steel mesh (a twentieth century renovation) wedged into the gaps. The log ends are half dove-tail notched to nestle and lock, one to the other above and below – passive, flexible, solid and durable. The logs represent the indigenous trees of the time, chestnut (before the blight), oak and white pine.

The original structure is sixteen feet deep by twenty feet wide (roughly five by six ax handles in the absence of a tape measure) with walls rising fourteen logs high (approximately fourteen feet). It was a one room structure with a loft, the floor of which was the ceiling of the main room and seven feet high. The front and rear walls had two windows and a door each. The south wall had two small windows on either side of the stone fireplace. Built in the mid-nineteenth century, it was originally home to the John Wright family, a family of eight.

Across the front of the cabin is a hip-roofed porch. A porch is a room with a single wall. A room where you can be outdoors without being exposed. A room that captures the slightest breeze, secure from rain but close enough to smell and even taste it. A place to meet and chat, to watch and pass the time in easy moments of thought without consequence. A place to dream. A place to wake. A place to rock and muse and meditate on the sounds of the wind and birds.

At some time in the past and now long gone, a kitchen shed was built onto the back of the cabin. You could still see the evidence of the roof line where there was old rot on the outside of the back wall above the porch. There would also have been an outhouse. Some people call an outhouse a privy; however, the phonetics of that nomenclature is too close to our family surname so we prefer outhouse. Of course, there are other options, most of which are either territorial or archaic: johnny, pot, latrine or throne.

In any case, the most interesting thing that could be found on the property other than the buildings that have survived or a gold mine would be the location of the outhouse. A snapshot of history, a subterranean vault of forgotten memories. A compost of human history, a trash pit, but from a time when everything inorganic was too precious to be discarded unless truly useless, broken beyond function or repair. A selective collection of period hardware, albeit embedded in the most personal of waste.

We never found the location of the outhouse. Likely it was hung over the creek for speedy elimination of waste, a modern precursor to enclosed sewer systems. Effective, if not entirely positive for the environment.

About 1952, the cabin was modernized. The

entire structure was taken apart and rebuilt. The original kitchen shed was demolished, and an ell ("L") addition was built along the east (back) and north wall. The addition provided for a kitchen with eating area, a bathroom and a bedroom. Various pantry and storage spaces were constructed that filled every available nook and cranny in a way reminiscent of the efficiency of a cruising sailboat. No space wasted.

The rear door of the original cabin became the doorway into the kitchen, and one of the windows a bookshelf between kitchen and family room. Another door opened from the kitchen onto a small back porch. The interior of the entire addition was paneled with white pine. It was raw wood when we lived there, though it may have been treated with linseed oil originally. The floors were also white pine, a native and readily available wood.

The loft floor (ceiling for the den) was raised in the renovation so that it is more than eight feet clear now. Similarly, the roof for the loft was raised so that it is more than eight feet at its highest, sloping to front and back with the roof line.

The old cedar shake roof was replaced with tin. The tin is now more than fifty years old.

The fireplace is stone, constructed of river rocks most likely from this land. It is built of mortared stone now, but the foundation below the hearth is dry laid without mortar to bind the stones. The internal foundation stones were also laid without mortar, but the perimeter stones have been cemented into place. Foundation stones, large slabs of river rock were dry laid under the perimeter sills.

Over the fireplace, the wood mantel extends the full sixteen foot depth of the cabin.

When we signed the contract for the purchase of the cabin, we naturally included a provision for having the structure inspected for deferred maintenance, leaking pipes, termites, moisture rot, broken toilet seats, sprung hinges, etc. Our inspector met me at the cabin after he had climbed and crawled and thoroughly, so I believed, turned the cabin inside out and learned all the secrets that the Sellers would have chosen to keep confidential. He declared the cabin in exceptional condition, for its age. He expressed surprise that there was no real structural damage, just a couple of floor joists under the kitchen that looked a bit weak from moisture and bugs: easily replaced if and when I chose. Nothing at all pressing. I paid him his fee and thanked him for easing my mind. We had cleared the only obstacle that had concerned me. If the cabin had been too far gone (though not to the eye), it might have been cost prohibitive to restore and adapt for our use.

Also part of the homestead were a hill house, a work shed, a garage (or tractor barn) and a livestock barn. The hill house (or spring house, we are not sure) was built into the side of the ridge just a few steps from the back door. It housed our washer, dryer and an extra refrigerator.

The work shed is out front to the left of the cabin. It is a rough and simple but sturdy design that seems to have been a place to store tools, work on farm implements and likely housed an animal such as a goat at one time as evidenced by some thoroughly chewed wall studs. We had the whole building rebuilt without refining it; the floorboards were left untouched, rough cut and uneven. Invisible behind the older frame, we had installed a new sill, a solid sleeper, and new exterior boards (wormy chestnut) cut from old barn lumber so that it looked just as ragged as before but without the rot that had begun to erode the planks from the foundation up. The over-sized front door was left with gaping spaces between boards, crooked on its tired hinges.

The tractor barn or garage had two bays and an open eave on the north end. From the road, you could see the dry laid stone foundation that supported the structure against the side of the creek bank. The floor was dirt. Although not as large as a modern garage, the bays were just wide enough for our vehicles with room inside to open doors, etc. Cozy but functional.

The barn is the jewel of the old homestead though. It is a three bay log structure with several adaptations over the years. The end bays were stalls. The center bay was not a stall but was converted to a stall by enclosing the open front at some point. The logs are mostly oak and chestnut; three of them extend the full length of the barn, approximately fifty feet. To the rear and above the log structure is a post and beam addition. On the eastern end is a shed roof.

As much as I loved the cabin at first sight, it was the barn that truly stole my heart. Seeing it across the unkempt upper pasture that first day, it languished in disuse; nevertheless, it anchored the north boundary of the property as a stately and stalwart reminder of better times, of times when this land was the productive farm and homestead that its owners had dreamed it would be. Surely a building as solid and enduring as such a barn would have encouraged the labors of a family that may have possessed little but knew they had much in the life they made on this place.

Buying a place such as that homestead connects you to history. Not the academic, big battleground kind of history, but the real and tangible human history of a place. The cabin is a very visible part of that history as are the other buildings on the land.

But there are other levels of that history that are not as visible. When we hiked through the woods or along the creek, we were mindful of loose and erratic strands of rusty barb wire. Those strands were sometimes buried in the growth of a large locust or oak. Some were attached, as they had been for over a hundred years, to locust posts that never rot. Some posts had fallen as if torn from the ground, but mostly they stood rough and roughly split where tired hands dug a posthole and set them decades ago. Evidence, artifacts, such as that grounded us in the real use of the land. A barrier for livestock, mostly cattle.

There were trees that had fallen, marking storms over the decades before our arrival. There was the occasional pot, pan or stove piece that turned up on the forest floor, disguised by rust, blending with the dusky duff, but revealed by a shape that was not truly of nature or the forest. There were rock piles that were not left behind by retreating glaciers. Bright quartz marked a gathering of stones from the pasture or some other clearing project. And there was the moss that covered most everything, proving that little had changed for a many years preceding our arrival.

We saw those things and realized that we wanted the moss to be part of us because we wanted to be a long time part of that place. We did not want to be the change that scrapes the moss from the stone. We did not want to be the fresh white cement that improved the old stone wall or chimney. We wanted to blend with and become a part of what was old and established and constant.

WHY MOVE TWO

Some friends wondered why we chose a change in lifestyle. Even more, they wondered how we left an urban center with all of its culture and activities to move to the country. I think the simplest explanation is that what we hoped to experience, and what we have experienced, was both richly diverse and elemental. Elemental and basic. Feeding a core need for what is true, the heart of our souls.

Even more than what the city offered was what we could find without ever leaving our home land. The cool dew of dawn between your toes, the comforting fragrance of morning fog in your nose. The tapping of rain on the tin roof. The chattering creek after a thunderstorm. Wild country, wild animals. Open land, forests, streams, brook trout and bears.

One night during our first week, Beth tried to wake me because she heard something ransacking our back porch. I muttered "okay" without waking, so she went downstairs to investigate. The back porch was lit; something had tripped the motion sensor light. Peering out the kitchen window, she saw a raccoon as big as a medium- sized dog scooping paws full of cat food into its mouth. She tapped on the window to scare it off; it stopped, looked around and continued eating, content to be our neighbor.

It was strange at first to live in a place that has historically been a vacation destination. It felt like skipping school, like getting away with more holidays than the company allows. Every day brought small wonders. The loud whistle of a pileated woodpecker (Woody) in the morning when it came to feed on the bugs in the fifty-foot dead trunk of the white pine beside our stone grill. Crawfish skittering under stones in the creek. The murmur of the creek in the still of night. Hooting barred owls and trilling screech owls. Black snakes, hawks, box turtles, grouse, great blue herons, bobcats and bears. The rush of water after a summer thunderstorm. The echo of thunder rolling up the cove. Rabbits. The invisible but unavoidable moles. Briars and poison ivy and poison oak. All manner of stinging insects (hornets and wasps of more varieties than I can name). Spiders in all forms from wolf to granddaddy longlegs (and several varieties of those as well). And wildflowers: jack in the pulpit, three varieties of trillium, touch-me-nots, asters, sunflowers and more.

The cabin was a simple joy. Old and weathered despite extensive repair. A leaky tin roof whose leaks were rarely in the same place twice. Even the porch roof leaked; at first there were two leaks, small drips from old nails, but each storm revealed new drips and forgot old ones. Every wood eating insect imaginable had enjoyed feasting on the logs over the years. When the (third) termite inspector came out, he remarked how easy it was to deal with the termites as compared with the powder post beetles (active or gone, we did not know), carpenter bees (we had a full colony buzzing about for a few weeks drilling holes in everything) and all the other little bugs that live to consume wood.

A new old home would not be complete without repair and renovation and the pleasures of all the work and expense. We had to replace the entire floor system of the fifty year old addition. That led to the selection of a knowledgeable local contractor, a man (or family of men in our case) who could do anything that can be done with a power tool, hammer and nail. A disappearing contractor, of course. [The contractor wanted to move to Montana where a man can be a man and no one tells him what to do, including his clients.] And a plumber/electrician who had decided he did not want to make a few thousand dollars for a couple days' worth of work that month after all, but would not return my calls to admit that he really did not want the work. Hell, as soon as I hired someone else, I knew he would find a gap in his busy schedule to fit me in. And he would be insulted that I did not think he was going to show up three or four weeks after he said he would.

We met a lot of friendly people, most of whom are transplants, escapees from the north or the coast or from Tennessee. We also met natives who resented the immigration of people like us, but who profited (from people like us) like never before in their lives. I called my friend Todd, a fourth generation native of these parts, repeatedly for lessons in mountain culture. I worked hard to tame my big city impatience.

We learned about local issues like No Zoning in Fairview ("No Means No" read all the hand-painted signs). If there was zoning, you could not locate a mobile home or mobile home park right next to your neighbor's half million dollar home without running the gauntlet of governmental approval. That might stifle a local's ability to profit. Worse, Les might have to move his Tree Service (sawmill) out from in front of his home beside Old Fort Road to an area designated for business. He'd have to commute. Not fair in Fairview. [In fairness to Les, he sold me a cord of firewood late one sub-freezing winter's night after he had worked a long day hauling timber to Rutherfordton, so I am eternally appreciative. Still, you get the idea.]

I enjoyed being able to justify the acquisition of manly tools and equipment. I bought a 17 hp lawn tractor (riding mower), which I purchased only to discover upon reading the Owner's Manual when it was delivered that it is expressly NOT suitable for the mowing of pastures, which is exactly what I bought it for. Then I proceeded to discover every single rock and stump in the overgrown pasture despite raising the blade to its highest setting. After the first round, the blades probably would not cut a stick of melted butter.

Of course, I tackled the briars with my new weedeater, which came with a brush cutting blade. I tried to destroy that the same way I terminated my mower blades, by cutting anything in my path, including, but not limited to, rocks, trees and old rebar fence posts. I removed the blade and switched to a standard nylon weedeating line until I destroyed that too. In the last episode of my land reclamation project, I weed-ate (sic) all the low growing brush I could swing the weedeater into. As the line stripped the weeds from the land, it spat a continuum of rocks, pebbles, shredded weeds and chunks of wood at high speed into my shins and calves. I fought bravely on, determined to clear the land of overgrowth, including an ancient and well-established crop of the aforementioned poison plants. Too late in the day, as I ran out of gas (me and the weedeater), I realized that perhaps clearing the land in short pants had not been the smartest idea. Three days later, thinking I had been attacked by a colony of chiggers, I discovered that I had a raging case of poison everything all the way up to my knees with a few places on my arms for effect. Bright red and insanely itching, no amount of scratching or alcohol (external or internal) gave relief.

I did however experience a belated epiphany. Left behind in the medicine cabinet by the previous owners were two antique bottles of a medicinal nature. One was clear with a faded label reading Witch Hazel;

sounded like an organic home remedy kind of thing to me. The other was a brown bottle of long-since-separated Calamine Lotion. My epiphany was this: both are key to the treatment of bad cases of poison anything.

Beth and our children adapted well. Our son and daughter liked playing in the cold water of the creek, climbing into the loft of the barn, pulling crawfish and rocks from the creek. Beth coped with the tiny kitchen mainly because we installed a beautiful piece of Juperano granite for a countertop; it had veins of quartz accented by black lines coursing through the reddish brown and gray stone. Though polished, it retained its soul as a rock, a slice of ancient boulder born in the volcanic explosion of a world long past. Beth showed the patience of a saint by washing our clothes at the laundromat for a few months until I could "fix" a laundry in the spring house (more on that later).

We set a couple of Adirondack chairs and a

picnic table in the side yard under an ancient black walnut tree with a wall of one hundred year old boxwoods creating an outdoor "room". In the early days, Beth and I ate most of our meals out there. At first, all of the falling green walnuts (except one) missed us, so we enjoyed the shade and the breeze. By fall, we needed helmets and shoulder pads.

We never named our homestead anything other than the Cabin. We thought of Privette Pastures but didn't like the monogram or the alliteration. Maybe it should have been Briarbank in honor of the thorny thickets of Cherokee primrose that lined the creek and the woods. I alone called it Mole Ranch to commemorate a population of three species of moles with numbers sufficient to keep the Brits in moleskin breeks for another generation or so.

FIRST NIGHT

We needed to sell our house in Atlanta before moving to the cabin so we agreed to rent the cabin until we could buy it. As soon as we had the papers signed and the tenant vacated the property, we planned a trip the first weekend in December. It was like camping out but with a cabin instead of a tent and a fireplace instead of a firepit.

I was already in Asheville on business, so Beth and our children drove up after school. Waiting for them had been like waiting for Christmas morning. With no refrigerator, I laid champagne in the creek to cool. I had prepared a menu to celebrate the first step in our emigration out of the city and back into our homeland.

As my family turned into the driveway, they saw smoke rising from the cabin chimney and an open fire blazing in the outdoor stone grill. Our two children spilled from the car, glad to be in the mountains at last.

"This is cool," our daughter declared with a big smile.

The sun drifted below the western ridgeline, and the early shadow of evening settled gently over the cabin and pastures. A sliver of moon braced the sky along with Venus and a star. Through the window, candles danced on the mantel. It was a welcoming end to the day, a hopeful beginning to our new lives.

Our son ran over to the stone grill and peered into the fire. He was curious because we had only gas logs in our Atlanta house; although he had seen fires when we camped, it was still something novel for him.

"What is this?" he asked.

"An outdoor grill," I replied.

"Wow."

"Let's go down to the creek." I led the way.

"What is it?" asked the kids.

Stepping down to the edge of the creek, I pulled from the chilly water a bottle of champagne for me and Beth and a bottle of sparkling apple juice for the kids. We returned to the cabin, clustered around the fireplace hearth and its happy fire and toasted the beginning of a new chapter in our lives.

"Cheers."

The floor of the family room sloped downward as it entered the kitchen. The floor of the kitchen rocked and rolled like a heaving sea. Old and incomprehensible angles formed the cabinets and countertops. I was sure that some of it had been a good idea at the time of its creation, but in the present could make no sense of it whatsoever. Our kids poked around the rooms, of which there were few.

"Where will we sleep?" they asked.

"On the floor in front of the fireplace."

They smiled at each other mischievously.

We boiled some rustic Italian pasta on the old electric range, finding that it heated better than any modern electric range and almost as well as a gas range. Olive oil, garlic and parmesan. A simple but filling pasta for a cold winter night in the mountains. Grilled salmon, asparagus. And an American Cabernet from Biltmore Estate, the antithesis of our cabin.

****

Two sounds were constant at the cabin: wind in the trees and water in the creek as it tumbled over rocks. The wind came and went, sometimes rattling gently through the poplars along the edge of the pastures, sometimes roaring down from the ridge and crashing into the cabin as if dropped from the sky.

Sometimes, it stayed high on top of the mountain and only its distant roar descended to us, sounding like a distant jet passing miles overhead.

The creek lived several different lives as it flowed across the front of our land. At our northern boundary, Trantham Creek emerged from our neighbor's land at the end of the state maintained road The creek entered a small stand of hemlock adjacent to the barn, a dark and green shaded nave with big rocks and a couple of pools large enough to support small fish. It was cool, inviting and peaceful. I stepped down rocks along the bank and immersed myself in its shadows, savoring the refreshing damp quiet air that, despite being beside the road, behind a screen of hemlocks was private and serene.

From the hemlocks, the creek dropped into a thicket, an inaccessible stretch of water until it passed under a fallen tree and spilled over a broad rock slab. As the creek rushed over the slab through rocks and splashed into still water below, it sang a bright song with a complexity of notes and varying rhythms. Partly surging, partly sighing, the creek broke into cheerful sounds.

That was the noisiest section of creek and the one that all of us, especially our dog, Scout, enjoyed most often. Except during summer dry spells, the creek above the cabin was at its deepest with smooth rocks covering the bottom. After running through the pastures or hiking up the ridge, Scout always hurried to his spot in the middle of the creek, dropped to his belly and, facing upstream, lapped the refreshing creek water. Likewise, after a good hike, I straddled the stream and scooped cool water over my face and head.

Leaving the slab rock behind, the creek spilled over a long gravel bar and then tumbled into a pool just below a large maple beside the tractor barn. Small trout huddled there. The run through the gravel rang a pitch or two higher than the upstream rapids. The symphony of water began to fill.

As it flowed past the tractor barn and under our

culvert and past a large black walnut perched on the lip of the bank, the creek pushed up against the rock wall bracing the road. Small, tight and overgrown with walnut, buckeye and wild cherry saplings as well as briars, that stretch of creek rushed and dropped through a few small pools, the sound contributing a muted background tenor to the louder upstream sections.

Below the tractor barn and the bridge, the creek bent into our land, leaving the roadside in favor of following an ancient and shaded lane at the bottom of the lower pasture. That was the pinch at the head of the lower cove where, before the state built a road up, the only passage into the upper cove and mountain beyond would have been immediately alongside the creek, probably along the old lane on the cabin side of the creek. That would have been the only level ground between the nose of two opposing ridges settling to the bottom of the cove from the east and the west. Alders line the creeksides like a primitive arch framing the sandy, mossy and rocky shore. After one more twist and pool, the creek left our land for our neighbors downstream.

SPRAWL

Sprawl is a fine word, a descriptive word. It is almost onomatopoeic; the sound of the word exposes the laziness that it defines. Sprawl is a tired word, tired like a beer-bellied good ol' boy collapsed on a sofa in front of a television. Sprawl is a word with nothing to recommend it, no redeeming qualities to provide a basis for a counterargument that "Sprawl is Good". Sprawl is the geographical equivalent of sloth.

So, why have so many of our fast-growing areas fallen ill with sprawl? Is it poor design? Lack of planning? Is it because the citizens of those areas like long commutes and congested roadways? Do they prefer the poor air quality that comes with slow moving cars?

Of course not.

Sprawl is a natural condition, much like gaining weight. No one sets out to create sprawl any more than we decide to gain weight. It happens over time, more through inattention than intent. But it happens.

Nevertheless, it is avoidable.

Looking at the dynamics of growth in our new home county, we can see the path to sprawl as plainly as if the Department of Transportation had already cut the right of way for a new highway. Unfortunately, just like the clear-cut right of way, the conditions for sprawl take hold long before the damage to the quality of life is universally apparent.

South of Asheville is a bucolic landscape of rolling hills and small valleys framed by the long ridges of Swannanoa Mountain, Burney Mountain and several smaller peaks. Despite having been settled over a hundred years ago, it has remained rural principally due to poor access. The Old Charlotte Highway cuts through the area. Originally known as Drovers' Road because it was the market trail from Asheville (and points north) to Charlotte, it was always a small, narrow and twisting mountain road that provided access over and through Hickory Nut Gap but not much else. The road was so difficult that Sherrill built an inn in 1854 to house travelers near the crest of the Gap, a day's journey from Asheville fifteen miles to the north. Still, the beauty of the countryside attracted settlers, farmers and, ultimately, vacation homes.

Then came urban workers wanting to live in the mountains while being close enough to commute to work. They could rent the vacation homes cheaply. The early urban immigrants were willing to endure the slow commute of traveling the winding narrow mountain highway; it was the path to their liberation from things busy and urban. It was like heading out of town on vacation, but it happened every afternoon. It fed their dream of retirement long before they could collect a pension. And so, slowly, without a shred of intent, the population of Fairview grew.

As more and more people moved into the area, more and more cars crowded onto the small and winding mountain roads. The daily commutes stretched a little longer, but no one minded most of the time because it was part of the leisurely lifestyle. During the summer tourist season, some days would be slower than even a casual lifestyle could endure. Then there would be the month in autumn when the leaves change and the roads slow to a stop as visitors attempt to examine every single falling leaf for the perfection and vibrancy of its color. The more brilliant the turning leaves, the slower the commute. Happily, winter always returned, restoring the area to an unhurried and easy pace.

As the travel became more troublesome, residents and tourists alike began to demand better roads. The state finally obliged with an extension of five lanes to replace the narrow two. This required the removal of a significant part of a mountain and rerouting of a large creek.

Once the state builds a five lane highway to replace the quaint country road, the momentum is irresistible. Realtors tout the improved (faster) access. Retailers begin to count rooftops and household demographics. A new shopping center with grocery store sprouts, then a convenience store or three (gas and sustenance for the commuters and tourists). Realtors tout the availability of goods and services, which brings more people needing goods and services. The cycle of commerce is complete and self-perpetuating. More breeds more. Demand breeds supply.

The new residents also want some of the mountain experience, but increasingly, they want it in manageable, even packaged, form. In other words, the early settlers wanted tracts of land for agriculture (room for cattle to graze and crops to grow), then later residents wanted tracts of land for privacy. Recent residents want just enough land to have some privacy but not so much that they have to worry who is poaching their deer. The price of the land has not changed for the buyer all that much; early buyers would have paid $50,000 for their land. Today, many will pay a similar amount. The difference is that the early buyer bought a hundred acres or more for that amount; today, it is a couple of acres. The recent buyer does not even want fifty acres, asking the realtor, "What would I do with all that land?" Density swells.

The new residents are a source of demand for county services and a source of tax revenue to meet that demand. But all people must be taxed equally, so the farmer who is holding his land for farming is being taxed as if he *could* sell it for residential lots. Burdened by higher taxes than his small farm can support, the farmer (or more often his heirs) takes the only course left to him; he sells off small sites for new residents. Large tracts begin to evaporate. More people and more density and more cars. The roads that served the farmers well begin to crowd with the new residents commuting to work, carpooling kids to school and competing with tourists during summer and fall. In short, the secondary roads begin to fill to capacity. The new residents, new taxpayers, demand more and better roads. Speculators and land investors buy tracts from farmers to capitalize on the growth of the area. In order to justify increasing prices for the tracts they buy, they need to sell more home sites. To sell more homesites, they need to sell smaller sites (land being a finite commodity). They also need to sell sites that were not previously marketable, sites too small to meet the requirements for a septic system. In short, they need sewer.

Sewer is the principal catalyst of sprawl. Roads facilitate sprawl, but people will sprawl without roads; they cannot sprawl without sewer. Sewer is the lifeblood of sprawl. The county may limit homesites to one per acre subject to the site being suitable for a septic system (and suitable can be stretched to the point of failure). With sewer to the same site, the county might approve four to eight single family homes or, as part of a larger acreage, sixteen or more multifamily units. The return to the county is phenomenal on its face: many multiples of the population that could live on the same site with septic. And property tax receipts increase commensurate with the density and population increase.

When a county looks for a smart way to support increasing demand for new homes, it looks for where it can lay the most sewer line for the least cost. Naturally, the equation is not quite pure economics as politically influential developers and land speculators petition for where the line can "best serve the county". The discussion about where sewer can and should go can lead to trading potential school sites for development rights. Once upon a time, this might have been considered bribery; now it is known as a proffer or concurrency.

None of this growth is as sinister as the newspapers or movies make it sound. In fact, many of the people that cause the growth are the same ones that scream for the improvements, the expansion (including paving) of roads, sewer and other utilities to accommodate the native residents as well as the immigrating taxpayers. The growth that evolves into sprawl is seemingly innocent and, in that way, insidious. In the absence of a plan (which is not necessarily the same thing as zoning), by the time a community reacts to the problems of growth, it has likely slipped far down the slope toward sprawl. Government by the people being what it is, in the time that it takes to recognize the need for a plan, craft an acceptable plan and adopt, then implement a plan, years (even decades) will pass. All the while, growth proceeds and the demand for improved services continues; sprawl sprawls. It becomes a matter of fixing problems that then exist because the problems were not anticipated early enough to avoid.

It is rare that a community has leaders with sufficient vision and foresight to prepare for the otherwise inevitable. But there are such leaders. Just as importantly, there are towns and cities that have faced the disease of sprawl and learned ways to combat it. For those communities still struggling to understand their options, we can learn from those communities that have trod the path before us.

WEATHER

Our first year, on the last Saturday in July, the temperature never rose above 70 at the cabin. The nights were cool with several mornings a chilly foggy 60. Yes, we cheated with a window air conditioner in the loft since the late afternoon sun broiled the tin roof. But often the clouds over the mountains shielded us from the heat. And the black walnut trees surrounding the cabin likewise shaded us when the heat of the day settled heavily over the cove. The last week of July, Beth and the kids telephoned me at work in Atlanta about lunchtime one day to let me know that they were sitting at the picnic table under the big walnut tree beside the cabin enjoying a bright sunny day with cool breezes and 68 degrees.

To deal with the anticipated heat of summer, we identified some stretches of the creek where we could rest sweaty bodies and heat-tired bones in the brisk, cool current. Sitting on a smooth submerged rock or a soft pebbly gravel creek bottom, heavy creek water running thickly over our legs. But, the fact of the matter was that it was rarely that hot. The kids played in the creek with our black Labrador, Scout, and Beth and I sometimes waded in. But no one felt the need to soak.

The Asheville area, like much of the rest of the South, had been in a long, four year, drought in the late 1990s. Until we moved into the cabin. Our summers were cooler than average with no days above 90 (really none above 85) as measured at Asheville, which was consistently warmer than in the cove. But, the humidity could still strain our emotions. Of course, our historical information was all anecdotal data gleaned from passing conversations with the guys who changed our oil at the Kounty (sic) Line convenience store, gas and service station as well as the kid who bagged our groceries at the Food Lion, and the sales associate selling air conditioners at Lowe's. Well, it was not quite scientific, but highly reliable reporting from the locals.

The hottest day of the summer our first year was August 8. The temperature at the cabin finally rose above 80, and the night barely sank below 70. With a rain storm in between.

True to summertime, we had a period of a few weeks of regular rain. Mostly afternoon thunderstorms. The first heavy rain was delightful; Beth and I stopped what we were doing and listened to the drumming of the downpour on our tin roof. Then we stepped out onto the porch and watched the rain bands sweep across the lower pasture. The color and texture of a good rain is something of comfort, especially when you depend on a well for water. I had worried that it would be just our luck that the well that had provided water for fifty years or so would suddenly drop below the end of the pipe that sucks the water one hundred feet to the surface.

As the rain seemed to end, I stepped again onto the porch to listen and heard a constant murmur, like a steady rain continuing to fall. Then I looked at the small puddles along the gravel drive and noticed that they were slick and still. I listened again and realized that I was hearing the creek in spate, louder than usual.

We had a few memorable deluges that swelled the creek into a noisy torrent. The first big flooding rain, I went to the bridge to see how high the water had risen and suddenly a section of telephone pole raced past downstream, bouncing in the muddy current and disappearing around the bend before I could say, "What was that?" The really good news was that the flood washed away all of the briars I had cut along the creek bank during the winter, something I expected would happen with the spring rains that never came.

We were grateful for the rain. After a few more

downpours, I stopped worrying about the well going dry.

During the worst of the storms, I began to worry about how we might escape the cabin when (if) the creek washed out the culvert (our bridge) and stranded us against the ridge. Mud puddles sprouted like wildflowers in spring. There was a trail of new mud at the bottom of the lower pasture where it washed down the mountain from the gravel roads up the mountain above us.

The biggest test of how high the creek could rise came in 2004 when our mountains were hit by a series of three hurricanes back to back. No one had seen that much rain since the Great Flood of 1916 that was caused by two hurricanes within a week of each other. Houses and bridges were swept away. People died in massive slides of mud and debris that stripped the mountains clean in long gullies. On the ridge above us, Flat Top Mountain recorded winds of 92 miles per hour.

Our creek never rose to the halfway mark.

Still, despite dodging floods, I started focusing on the need to replace the roof. Like the cabin and the porch, the roof began to show its age after the passing of the first winter. What seemed to be a fairly reliable roof when we initially inspected the cabin began to look like the early stage of a skin disease with scabs of silver and rust peeling off a pitted surface.

When the rains came, we discovered a few leaks in the loft and a couple over the front porch. While not surprising, neither were expected based on the winter rains and snows we had seen. There had been no leaking then.

On the other hand, there was obvious staining on the tongue-and-groove paneled ceiling in the loft. The broker said it was the result of squirrels making a nest above the ceiling many years previous. While we did not entirely believe that, we did not think that there were active leaks. [As a footnote, neither did our house inspector think there was any active leaking, but then he thought the floors that were sagging and bouncing were structurally sound. We replaced the flooring system and sub-floor in its entirety. When I brought this to his attention, he admitted I was probably correct that he should have caught the deficiency, but he never offered to refund the fee I paid him for his "expertise".]

Anyway, we had a rainy day game anyone could play for free. Find the new leak. All the new leaks were actually old leaks, so the game was easy; look for the old stains and see if they glisten. If there were sparkles dripping to the floor, we placed a towel beneath them and looked for the next one. Occasionally the tap-tap-tapping of drips onto a cardboard box revealed a fresh leak hiding in the shadows.

The porch was a world of leaks that was even harder to follow. First were the two leaks I mentioned above. Then there was another and another. Then the deluge and there were several. With luck, as the deluge diminished, the nail holes would swell shut and the leak would disappear until the next fresh rain. But sometimes it just dripped like it was raining up under the porch roof. Good thing we kept the umbrellas in a crock by the front door. In case you wanted to sit on the porch during a rainstorm.

I contacted a roofing contractor who swore he was an experienced tin roof guy. He sounded like it and he may have been, but he did not show up. When I called him a week later, he admitted that he remembered me, remembered that we were supposed to meet the previous week, told me all the things that were not going right in his life and promised to get to me by middle of the following week.

Months passed without a word from the tin roof guy. I had another name to call, but became anxious about repeated rejection.

In addition to keeping dry, we also thought it important to keep warm during the cool nights of fall and spring as well as the frigid days and nights of winters that can freeze the creek solid. The stone fireplace was well-built and drew nicely.

However, remembering that the garage was filled with spruce split for firewood, and knowing that spruce, like pine, burns at low heat with heavy creosote build-up, I feared that the chimney might need a good cleaning. When I noticed what appeared to be smoke leaking from the chimney under the eaves, I feared that the chimney may have been cracked by the raising of the rear wall of the cabin and decided I should call an expert to evaluate the options. I called a licensed chimney sweep.

Unlike some of the other tradesmen, the chimney sweep did show up, and on time. He was delightful, knowledgeable (but I am easy to impress) and informative.

After taking a slow look up the chimney from the firebox, we went outside to look at the condition of the stone and mortar. He declared the chimney solid and remarkably good for its age. But…

"In its current condition, although structurally sound, it is not at all safe. Even if you didn't think that you might have a crack in it, I would tell you that you need to line it to operate it safely," he reported authoritatively. "You are a chimney fire waiting to happen."

"Well, I thought a lining might be one solution (as if I knew anything at all), so what will lining it cost me?" I liked the fact that we were cutting to the chase and moving on toward a solution. After all, this guy had shown up, knew what he was doing, was ready to make a recommendation on the spot and I might even get an estimate without giving him a chance to leave the property never to be seen by me again.

"We use seamless stainless steel and fill the cavity with stainless fiber insulation. It takes a lot to work a flue down an old chimney like that; the inside is likely to be very irregular with lots of twists. We can't just drop it in. $3,000. At least."

I gasped, and he heard me.

"Or, for the same, maybe less, I can install a

wood stove, complete with 6 inch flue."

"But my wife and I like the fireplace and really planned to suffer through being cold this coming winter so we could enjoy a real fire unconstrained by a stove. I was looking forward to waking every morning to a cold fireplace and fumbling with numb fingers as I tried to stack the kindling and light the match for a brand new fire that I then had to watch and nurture all day long so that we would have one warm corner of the cabin and so that I would not have to start the fire for a second or third time the same day. My wife and I like to sleep with it cold, and with a fireplace I knew I could count on the loft being as close to freezing as is possible in a home that has heat. The cold loft would justify buying thick down comforters, duvets, fleece throws, quilts, heavy flannel sheets, any number of bedroom items that a warmer home does not need." (I didn't really say that, but that's what I was thinking as I considered his suggestion.) Who needs the romance anyway? We had been married more than 10 years, had two children and were wondering if we would ever enjoy retirement since I would be over sixty when our youngest graduated college.

Oh well, he sold me on the wood stove. Which was like a lot of good decisions in life, he simply convinced me to be smart.

We looked forward to being cozy, if not entirely romantic, in winter.

While weather roughly follows calendar seasons, there were other seasons embedded within the calendar and weather. For both flora and fauna, there had been a variety of seasons with which we were not familiar.

First came the stinging insects (none of which bothered to sting us). There were hundreds of wasps, hornets and bees hovering and buzzing about. The insects had a habit of touching a surface (sometimes including skin or hair) ever so lightly and lifting immediately as if burned by the contact. Only the carpenter bees landed for any length of time, and their sole objective was the consumption of timber, of which the cabin had plenty despite the feasting of wood-eating insects for over a century.

We kept our eyes on the hornets and wasps, knowing that they would build nests at some point, vigilant to prevent the nests from becoming too large. I found, during the course of one summer, a few golf ball size hornet's nests and one the size of a softball on steroids. It was from this nest that we suffered our only casualty: Cameron was sitting with us under the shed at the barn when a flying insect shot out of the shadows, stung him painfully on the back of his buzz-cut head and retreated as swiftly as it had charged. Though Cameron cried, there was no significant damage.

A few wasps nests in the barn, garage and shed along with some mud-daubers' tubes in the garage.

I was certain there must have been at least one hornets' nest of impressive size somewhere in the woods above the cabin. I searched the empty trees on cold winter walks, but never found one.

After the stinging insects, whose visits lasted a couple of weeks or so, there emerged a veritable plague of granddaddy longlegs. Hundreds if not thousands. Red bodies, orange bodies, brown bodies. Some large, some medium, some small. The colors of the bodies probably correlated to size and species differentiation, but I was just not that interested in being able to discern what was what in the granddaddy longlegs world. It might have been revolting if not for the fact that all of us, except Cameron, will take a longlegs over a web spider any day.

Cameron developed a toxic fear of granddaddy longlegs during a summer overnight rafting trip on the New River in West Virginia. Good friends from Atlanta had asked us to join them. At the end of a day's float, we stopped at a wide beach in a bend of the river. We spotted the spiders all around the sandy riverside camp site, but thought little of it, failing even to zip the tent door closed. After a delicious camp meal and good conversation by the campfire, all retired to their tents to sleep or read. Soon after I turned off my headlamp, a shrill and terrified shriek ripped through the tent. A granddaddy longlegs had dropped from the ceiling onto Cameron's face; it was worse than a nightmare to wake with the legs stretched over his eyes and nose.

Everywhere we sat in the side yard of the cabin, we were visited by longlegs. On the Adirondack chairs, the table between the Adirondack chairs, the picnic table, the picnic table benches. We picked them off wine bottles and juice glasses, dinner plates and hors d'oeuvres.

There seemed neither rhyme nor reason to their actions other than to be anywhere and everywhere at once. Unlike the other insects, the population of longlegs seemed to diminish only slightly over time. It was early autumn before the longlegs were finally scarce.

On the other hand, the spiders were extremely active in the autumn as the leaves began to change. During the summer, we had rarely found a real spider web. Then suddenly, the week after Labor Day, there were webs and egg sacks under all the eaves. And big writing spiders stringing their magnificent webs from the boxwoods alongside the cabin.

Taylor and a friend took a hike through the woods in late November and came face to face with many old webs. It lasted little more than two weeks; the spiders had laid their eggs, eaten a few bugs, had their webs wrecked by longlegs accidentally trapped and disappeared for another winter.

In late summer, fireflies emerged from the pastures at dark, rising like galaxies of stars into the night sky.

By mid-September, the heat vanished in the cool breezes that were harbingers of fall. Days were sunny and clear, beautifully pleasant. Nights were cool, dipping into the 40s. We usually fired up the wood stove for its inaugural by September 15, the first cold morning after summer. The cabin warmed slowly with a modest fire. Then we opened the windows at the end of the day until the night brought cold air. It was like living outside with doors and windows open during the day and night. Buried under fleece blankets, we slept, cozy under covers.

In October, the lady bugs hatched and floated over the pasture like fairies in the afternoon sun. Inside, they were an epidemic pox of crawling orange dots along the windowsills and floors.

Then the black walnuts fell. Continuously for a more than a month.

I almost stepped on the only copperhead we ever saw. He was lazing at the corner of the garage. Tom, who owns the bottom land cow pasture along Cane Creek at the foot of Wright's Cove, advised that he only saw snakes in March and September: emerging from hibernation and preparing to hibernate respectively. Both were times that snakes tended to be irritable. Although we were committed to living with all the native creatures, the exceptions were poisonous snakes as well as mice and spiders inside the cabin. But then, we never could keep the mice or spiders out of the cabin.

One morning, taking a break from working on the computer, I looked out the loft window into the upper pasture and saw a great blue heron standing proudly beside the well head. He spooked when he spotted me trying to sneak into the shed to tell Beth and the children.

Fall was the season of relief as we escaped the humidity of summer and returned to the do-anything perfection of cool, dry weather. The nights dropped into the forties (some in the thirties); the days followed with a penetrating chill until midday when Indian summer visited for the last several hours of daylight. The sun fell below the western ridge of the cove about 5:30. Then the cold night air seeped back in.

The trees began changing late September. First a hint of tentative yellow from the poplars, then brilliant red from the maples. Overnight, the yellow became gold, then orange. The mountainsides were radiant with the warm colors of autumn in the soft light of sunset. The night sky was so clear that the stars seem to hover at the top of the ridge, just out of reach. Cold weather brought a clarity of sight and thought. A clarity of feeling.

Fire in the woodstove. Hot tea after breakfast. Something about the comfort of heat when it is cold that makes life feel just right. Something about walking through the pasture or the woods after hearing the nightly news that made life at the cabin feel just right. Learning to savor the unpredictable and uncontrollable elements of weather and the movement of seasons was the adventure of waking every morning to a new day.

A month into autumn, the forecast called for clear skies and mid 50's and a low in the upper 20's. The skies never cleared for more than a few minutes at a time, so the high was about 48. And breezy.

Les, the wood guy, delivered a cord in late afternoon. He hails from South Dakota where it gets really cold. I asked him if it was a bit cool for this early in autumn. He declared the cold winds "wicked".

We had invited some friends for a bonfire party. The wind almost prevented the lighting of the bonfire, but the winds dropped enough to have a safe smaller bonfire. Good friends visited the cabin for the first time and enjoyed a low country boil. Not sure why we thought seafood made sense for a mountain cabin party, but it was tasty.

My good friend, Michael, visited from Atlanta, exploring the woods up high with his dogs. When he returned, he wanted to "do something physical", like stack the wood. As we began to stack the wood, the clouds darkened, and it snowed the first snow of the season.

Winter is the season when the skin of the earth is revealed in the mountains. You can look through the forest that masks the land and its shape much of the year. You see wrinkles and folds like furrows in an old man's brow. You see the evidence of age, the cuts and breaks and tumbled boulders of prehistoric change.

You see stones worn smooth by patient time.

Our mountains express themselves as subtle drama. The Appalachians are ancient, as old as any mountains in North America and some of the oldest on the planet. Theirs is not the drama of a glacier grinding inexorably to the sea, but the drama of storm, season, time. It is the drama of us all where any one of us may be the storm and some of us will be the season. The series of all of us will be time itself.

I liked the changes of terrain, where a gently rolling valley floor lifts to meet the steepening ridge or cliff face. I imagined the timeless forces that began with violent collapse – a rock face suddenly sheared free -- evolving into an invisible aging of time and river, soils lost and regained. It is change so subtle that we can measure it only by comparing present to distant past, a change measured in generations, not seasons or years.

With the coming of spring, the mountains brightened with fresh spring leaves sprouting new and tender, brightly green from trees that were gray and lifeless just a month before. Rain and sudden storms materialized from nothing, emerged without warning from cool air that reminded us how recently passed was winter. Other days, the air was motionless and humid, promising summer.

Wildflowers dappled the roadsides and paths. Dogwoods splattered soft white blossoms through the woods. Butterflies and nesting birds fluttered. Young squirrels dashed about madly. Spring was a season promising with new life.

Open windows drew soft, quiet, fog-laden dawn. Our senses reconnected with birdsong and the sweet fragrance of new grass. The creek tumbled lively as if freed of the threat of a winter freeze. Rising and falling with sudden rain, the creek lifted its voice in a song that celebrated the young and hopeful, a release from winter's monochromatic silence.

We woke to the clear and insistent symphony of songbirds around the cabin. The music of joy. In the early dawn, the cove was barely lit by the expectation of the sun rising far over the mountains to the east. A gentle fog rested over the pastures and woods, cool and soothing as if intended to ease us into the day.

One part of me wanted to turn over and snuggle deeper into warm sheets. A bigger part of me wanted to be part of each new day, to see, hear, smell and taste a time made rare by the sleep of our neighbors, the quiet absence of human activity. The wild world awoke and I yearned to be part of it.

One morning, before the first brightening of dawn, a murmur pressed down the mountain and over the woods. The gentle and patient static of rain. With the comforting blur of sound, I turned over and burrowed more deeply under the flannel sheets and wool blanket. A rush of wind swept over the cabin and burst into the open windows. Cool, fresh and excited air whispered its invitation to wake and get an early start on the day. Rise! Bundle up and settle into a rocking chair on the porch. Watch, listen, smell and feel the rain and the rainy fresh breeze. Rock contentedly as the sky brightens with the rising of the sun beyond the clouds. Watch the pasture slowly emerge as if materializing out of darkness. Hear the wind spilling through the trees. Hear the chatter of the swelling creek. Smell sweet mown grass. Smell clean cold rain. Feel rain's chill breath as the wind sweeps it under the eaves, dampening the porch and chairs.

As much as spring is a time of life, part of living is dying. In the course of one twenty-four hour period, Harley (our cat) killed and ate a mouse, killed and ate a blue jay and killed a mole. He would not eat moles; they must have tasted bitter. In the barn, Cameron found the carcass of a devoured young squirrel. Taylor heard the desperate cries of a bird being killed up in the woods—whether by snake, hawk or cat, we did not know. But when we watched the downy feathers drift on the breeze out over the pasture, we suspected a broad wing hawk had shocked its prey mid-air, then perched on a high branch to pluck and dine.

On the other hand, rabbits (and likely snakes, field mice, turtles etc.) thrived in the high cover of the unmown pasture.

All in all, spring was a confusing opportunity. Days were warm, but cool. Nights were cool, but warm enough to sleep with windows open. Spring was the best of a mild winter mixed with a mild summer. Spring was a season of surprise. Maybe winter. Sometimes summer.

It was the promise of a pleasant, warming season as dogwoods budded and daffodils bloomed. It was the sobering cold of a winter storm surging northward with snow the day after bright sun and temperatures in the high fifties. Each clear and sunny day we believed that spring had sprung, and we prepared to drift into summer. Then damp, drizzly, snow flurry days reminded us that winter had not yet surrendered.

Soon, it was the first of June and high winds mark the passing of a cold front. Cold wind poured through open windows in our loft, leaving dreams of the next autumn. Despite feeling like the beginning of spring, the calendar said that summer was just around the bend of a few weeks' time. And yet the temperature at night tumbled into the 40s. We had had a fire in the woodstove every week since April.

FIXIN' UP

The first electrician (who was also a licensed plumber, which distinguished him from many of the people recommended to us as reasonably priced, but possibly under-skilled) agreed to do some renovation work ($3,000, which I thought might hold his attention) and even came to the cabin once to help with a "plumbing problem".

I thought the steadily dwindling water pressure was a fairly easy thing to fix since it seemed to occur only in the kitchen. Of course, I could not figure it out for myself since I am a mechanical idiot. Turns out it was simply a matter of the screen filter in the sink faucet being clogged with junk from the water pipe. It took the electrician/plumber less than five minutes to "fix". Appreciative, I learned a new skill in the process.

Still, I never saw the electrician/plumber again. He never called to say he did not want the work, never said boo.

More importantly, he never installed the new meter base for increased electrical service; we were upgrading from 60 amp to 200 amp. No modern home has less than 100. Even though fuses are better than circuit breakers, they are somewhat anachronistic today. The power company's underground installation crew showed up and declared they could not dig the new line because they did not know where the meter base was going to go, as if we might relocate the whole electrical service to an entirely different wall of the cabin when all the internal wiring already feeds to a fifty year old meter on the north wall. In other words, even though it was clear that the new meter would be in exactly the same location as the current meter.

They rescheduled the installation. The

electrician did not reschedule. He was nowhere to be found.

Once again, I searched for a reliable and reliably skilled electrician to perform the necessary upgrade. I found one. I am not sure how. Blind luck through the Yellow Pages, believe it or not. You know the saying about a blind hog finding an acorn once in a while.

After two days, I gave Henry (not his real name) a draw against work completed, and he promised to return after the County Inspector checked the new service for code compliance. I made sure Beth had plenty of cookies, an apple pie and a freshly baked chocolate cake on hand as well as hot fresh Starbucks coffee to wash it down; we wanted to cover all the bases since we did not know what county inspectors in this part of the world cotton to.

I do not know which did the trick, but we passed our inspection. The rest of the work was done "underground", so to speak, which is to say without governmental oversight.

Henry lived in a nearby town, not so near as the first electrician, but Henry showed up when he said he would and returned to complete all the work. Henry even hired our son to assist him running wire under the cabin and paid him for his time. He was a soft-spoken, friendly man who joined us for lunch at our picnic table under the black walnut. He seemed genuinely to enjoy the company and conversation.

The hill house was not a building per se since it was built into the side of the ridge. It was like a spring house; however, spring water no longer bubbled up and flowed through. We thought the spring water was still there. It was, unfortunately, hidden under a slab of concrete. And the walls were concrete block instead of stone. The temperature was fairly constant and cool, even with summer and opening the doors every day. In winter, we never had anything freeze in the spring house, even though temperatures dipped into the single digits at night and did not rise above twenty-five degrees for several days.

While the old timers used a spring house as their refrigerator, we mimicked them by keeping an extra refrigerator in our hill house. We also modernized it with power and plumbing for use as storage and laundry. There was an outlet already in place, but the dryer needed 220, so we had Henry run that from the main box underground to the spring house.

Eventually, the power company sent a crew to bury our power line to the cabin underground. They warned me it would leave a mess of a ground scar. They were excessively correct. The mud I expected. The stones, rocks and boulders I did not. Admittedly, I should have known that they would dig up a few rocks because we have a healthy crop of them all around the property, mostly in convenient and out of the way places. However, nothing prepared me for the volume of stones removed or the size of some of the boulders that they failed to return to the ground.

Now, stones I could load in the wheelbarrow and collect for deposit in a place of my choosing. But the boulders were another matter all together. The smallest was about two feet diameter and granite; the prettiest was somewhat longer and solid quartz. In neither case could I move the boulder. And of course, there was the enduring mystery of volume; how can one remove more dirt from a hole than it takes to refill it? I had five medium-sized boulders no longer embedded beneath the surface, but the trench from which they were dug was full.

On the bright side, having boulders that need to be relocated was a manly opportunity. Clearly a new piece of equipment was needed, a front loader maybe. Or at least a small bobcat with a shovel attachment. If I was going to dig my own trenches in the future, I would need the trenching attachment as well.

Once Henry's work was complete, I called a plumber to run a line from the cabin to the hill house. The plumber said he could not come for four weeks. I told him that I could live with four weeks, but not more. After I described what we needed (extend the water pipe from one corner of the spring house around to the other side for a washer connection), he said he would try to come the week following our conversation. Of course, he did not come, nor did he call.

Same with the roofer. I could have called any roofer in the Yellow Pages if we had typical asphalt shingles; every bubba and his brother (who may be his cousin) could do asphalt shingles. No, I had to find someone who knew how to use tin. I needed someone who knew how to install tin roof properly, unlike the hacks that installed it originally who failed to maintain the shingle of one panel over the one below it. So, the existing roof looked like a bad mountain quilt, which would have been lovely if it had not been a roof and if the roof had not been leaking due to the quilting. There are many more ways to mess up a tin roof than an asphalt roof. I did not know why or all the details, but I knew it was true. Lots of people told me so.

At last, I found a tin roof contractor who had been in business about twenty years. He should have known what he was doing, so I called him on the phone and he told me all the things going wrong with his business: two trucks down (I think he owned two trucks, so he had none in service), rain ("can't roof in the rain") and inexperienced crews that he could not release unsupervised (and I was wondering why he would want to not supervise). We scheduled a time that was convenient to him, and he did not show. Nor did he call.

I was getting accustomed to that treatment; I was taking it less and less personally. Still, I hoped that the roofer might remember and call even if it was late. After a week, I called him again. He remembered me; he even found his notes with my phone number and address. He told me he was still having troubles, but hoped he could make it the following week. Now, bear in mind, he was not coming to do the work; we were just trying to find a time for him to scope the project and maybe give me a quote before the entire cabin fell apart from wood rot. He promised to call.

Of course, he never did.

In the meantime, I found a log cabin renovation expert. We needed to replace or repair a rotten bottom log on the front at the level of the porch. We also wanted to replace the porch and the porch posts (which were the full diameter trunks of small trees, two of which were rotting badly at the base). We intended to replace the posts with locust and the porch with tongue-in-groove pressure treated lumber.

As for the log, I was scared we were going to have to find an old log structure and buy the whole thing or pilfer a good log that might fit. The expert said that was not necessary. He had done the evangelist Billy Graham's cabin and he could simply inject a material into the rotten log that would seal it and make it structurally reliable if not entirely sound. Not replacing a bottom log sounded good to me, so he said he would research it some more and get back to me in a few days. I never heard from him again.

Maybe I was rushing things. I apparently lacked the patience and appreciation of slower times, of smelling the roses, of postponing until the point of desperation everything that could be postponed.

I tried. I swear I did. But I had enough trouble pushing through my own projects. Thus, I knew how important it was to get things started so that the distant future would not suddenly become the recent past, and nothing had happened in between.

Carpe diem. For sure.

One of our new lessons was in the management of waste. We had a private garbage company; we were limited to one ninety-six gallon trash bin per week. Everything inside the trashcan was required be in a trash bag. No loose trash in the trashcan. No random cardboard boxes by the road. And positively NO APPLIANCES EVER.

When we moved in, we had a ton of old farm garbage that we needed to remove, including the wonderful 1950's vintage Universal electric stove we had replaced in the kitchen. I thought about loading the Land Cruiser and heading for the county dump, but soon realized it would begin an endless trek to and from the dump. Thus, another solution needed to be found. A dumpster! The "tool" *par excellence* of serious contractors and renovators everywhere. Not as pleasing as a manly tool, but it demonstrates to your neighbors that you are not messing around. You are playing with the big boys. They can tell that you are engaged in a serious project when they see that big brown rectangular tub of steel gracing your yard.

The last weekend in July, we filled a dumpster with sundry cast away items. Steel fence stakes from the last time someone had a horse or cow in the pasture. A chain link kennel door still bolted to a galvanized post (concrete attached). Steel fire door that seems to have come from an old factory and had no use at the cabin. A pitching net. Miscellaneous lumber long since rotten. Birds' nests of tangled barbed wire and electric fence wire: galvanized, aluminum and rusty steel. A bookcase of soggy composition board. Old hoses. The top half of a basketball goal and pole (to which was attached a softball-sized hornets' nest, still humming with activity.)

Leather gloves, dirt and sweat.

As good as it felt to have removed the unwanted and untrashable from the garage and behind the shed, it looked as if nothing much was done since there was much more to do. Most of the remainder could be burned and became the fuel for a bonfire.

And we kept the old electric stove. They would not permit us to put a stove in a dumpster. Kind of like family if you think about it.

The plumber never showed, never called. I am sure he has since made more money than he ever imagined possible and has retired to the islands to clip coupons.

But not me. I still had to produce a laundry.

Failing to find a plumber willing to work for pay, I ran out of options. Beth and the kids had been patient about exploring the wonders of the Oakley Coin Laundry (and it *was* great, for a laundromat). However, too much of anything is, well…too much of anything. So, it came time that something had to be done about having onsite laundry facilities.

Early on, I had suggested that the inside laundry room (with a stacked washer and dryer before us) be reclaimed as a pantry.

Beth thought that was a great idea, but then asked, "So where will the laundry be?"

"The spring house," I declared, with a proud smile. Proud at the spur-of-the-moment stroke of genius I had displayed with my creative solution. "There's already water and power to it."

"There is?" Her look said that my stroke was a stroke, but without the genius.

"Well, the light works, but not the water. I am

sure that we just need to find the valve that turns the water on." I did not entirely believe that it would be that simple, but that was my story. You know, once I said it, I had to stick to it.

My plan had been to find a knowledgeable plumber who would crawl underneath the cabin without fearing any snakes that might be hiding in the shadows and locate the winterizing valve that I hoped was the key to a fresh flow of water to the spring house. (No way I would go under the cabin before the temperature dropped below freezing.)

The plumber did not happen, so my time for hiring a solution began to expire as autumn arrived with cold nights and colder winds. The laundry room became my problem. And I had to act quickly before the harmony in our domestic affairs turned sour.

Now, I have always been a self-confessed mechanical idiot. I worked at a gas station my senior year in high school (during the 1973-74 gas shortage, a demanding job for sure). Do you think I learned how to do anything to a car besides change the oil and check the tires? Nope. Not me. I helped remove and repair water pumps, carburetors, all manner of greasy, dirty auto parts. I learned zip, nada. Except that GoJo is really great for removing gas and oil and grease from your hands. Of course it smells like Noxema blended with kerosene. But it really makes your skin sparkle. In fact, it will take the tan right off.

I recognized and embraced my opportunity to learn a bit of plumbing.

I knew some of the basic physics of plumbing. Water will not flow uphill of its own accord. I knew that the pipe joints need to be sealed, soldered, welded, cemented tight against potential leaking. I did not know HOW to do that, just that it seemed to be something that plumbers did.

To complicate matters, the draining of the washer to any place other than a septic tank -- a "gray water" system among the environmentally conscious, but self-sufficiently practical -- was a violation of local ordinance. Of course, the people we bought from (and the husband was a real plumber who worked for money; not for me, but for somebody) had run a PVC drain line from the pantry washing machine down the outside wall of the cabin and across the side of the cellar door. The water drained onto the ground of the side yard. Yep, right there on the ground, fresh and colorful, wet lint.

At least their drain line was close to the septic tank. The one I needed to run from the spring house was on the other side of the cabin. I decided to run it down to the pasture below the boxwoods.

That was about a forty foot run. Should I, could I, dig a trench that far? No way. Not with the crop of rocks in the ground that I mentioned earlier. Plus roots. I was mostly worried whether I could dig a deep enough trench to get down to where the drain would have to penetrate the spring house wall (below grade). Then, would I have enough drop in the line for it to actually drain as far as I wanted? It seems water wants to flow downhill.

After weeks of agonizing in ignorance over the details of something about which I knew nothing useful (the entire science and mechanics of constructing a plumbing system), I decided the only way to proceed was to proceed.

I drove to Home Depot and parked myself in the plumbing materials aisle and waited for a skilled employee to come tell me what I needed. Waiting, I wandered up and down the rows of pipe, fittings, more pipe, cements (glues), hoping to begin to frame some kind of understanding. PVC, copper. All sizes, diameters, lengths. Some white, some gray, some black. Of course, the copper was all copper. As I studied box after box of plumbing stuff, I realized that I was learning absolutely nothing. It made no sense to me. Just parts is parts.

I told the Sales Associate what I was trying to do. Of course, I lied about draining a washing machine by telling him it was a utility sink; I really didn't want to run the risk that he would decline to advise me if he knew I was installing an illegal system. And he helped me buy stuff that at least would fit together. You know, the correct diameter pipes with the same diameter fittings. Cement to attach the stuff. I had real doubts that I would remember what fit into what by the time I drove the ten minutes back to the cabin; I should have taken notes, or, better yet, recorded him on video.

Amazingly, the best part of the adventure was that it did not cost much, maybe forty dollars. That alone was a reason for jubilation given the cost of most of my experiments and renovations.

Back on the ranch, I armed myself with a new three pound hammer (miniature sledge hammer) and a cold chisel. I had no idea why they call it a cold chisel; it was some kind of durable steel and steel is cold, but I did not know. Shooting glasses protecting my eyes (since I had no goggles per se), I set the chisel against the concrete block wall of the spring house and began to bang away with the hammer. Carefully I banged a circle into the concrete block high up on the wall where I had decided the dryer should vent. Unfortunately, that particular block turned out to be a small half-block that was 100% cement with no internal cavity like a normal concrete block. So, I stopped before I destroyed the whole block and started another circle in a larger block and found my way inside by use of hammer and chisel and force.

Soon I had a hole the appropriate diameter for the dryer vent hose. Life was looking good. I was not yet a real plumber, but I had managed to complete one small step toward making the hill house a laundry room.

Hunkering down with shoulder to the side of the washer, I strained and pushed and managed to slide, or rather scrape and grind, the heavy machine across the concrete floor of the hill house. Then I placed chisel to wall and hammered another hole down low on the wall where I thought a drain line might work. In a matter of fifteen or twenty strokes of the hammer, I had punched through both the interior and exterior sides of the concrete block.

Of course, there was only dirt on the other side of the wall since I had not yet excavated the trench for the outside drain line. I pulled the shovel from its resting place just inside the spring house door and began to dig. The challenge was this: the hill house was built into the side of the ridge. A small rock wall about two feet high ran out from the stone front of the hill house, holding back the side of the ridge. At the side of the hill house, the hillside was between two and five feet high. Therefore, to dig to the level of the intended drain line, and to have a slope from the drain line to the pasture along the back of the rock wall, I had to dig below the level of the top of the wall. I mention this not because the digging is any more difficult than digging a trench at ground level, but only because it is more difficult to slope it without digging down three feet or more for a distance of, say, forty feet.

Down and down, excavating fist-sized rocks

from the small trench. Shoveling the dirt into the wheel barrow; I had decided that the excavated dirt would make good fill in the front yard where the bare soil from the burying of the power line still sagged, sadly covered with small rocks but no grass. After a few large wheel barrow loads of dirt, I smiled at my progress and suddenly realized that I had a sizeable trench and no dirt with which to refill it. Oh well, I thought, one problem at a time.

It was time for the plumbing. I had purchased about fifteen feet of rigid white PVC, 100 feet (the shortest length they would sell me) of flexible black PVC, assorted fittings (the purpose and positioning of which I prayed I would remember), a steel clamp, concrete screws, a wall bracket and a package of pipe cement: two four ounce cans, each with a purpose. While those were the smallest cans available, I soon discovered that they would provide me with three or four generations worth of PVC cementing at the pace of plumbing I intended to pursue.

I opened the can of "primer", a watery purple liquid lacking any substance whatsoever. Then I opened the can of cement, a proper glue that was thick and translucent. I cut the first couple of pieces of PVC and applied the purple primer, which left the pipe with a thin purple coat that dried quickly in anticipation of the cement that I applied next. Then I twisted the two ends of the PVC together in what I hoped was a perfect union, a seamless joint of everlasting durability, a flawless cementation of plastic to plastic. Anyway, what I hoped was that it stuck enough not to leak the first time water flowed through it.

Measure, cut, cement, twist. I pushed the stub of the P trap (did not know where they got that name either; maybe it was obvious as a plumbing term and I was in denial) through the back wall and into the open air. With a 22 degree angle connector, I linked the P trap to the eight feet of rigid white PVC running along the bottom of the trench. Then another connector designed to link (with a stainless clamp) the rigid PVC to thirty feet of flexible black PVC that ran the remaining distance to the edge of the pasture.

Done! Piece of cake.

Of course, for your benefit, I have edited and omitted the mistakes and false starts, the inevitable returns to Home Depot for other parts and more coaching.

And did it work? Well, that is my story. A little leak here, a little leak there. The washing machine washed clothes and the dryer dried them. Sounds like it worked to me.

WILDLIFE

Before we closed on the purchase of our cabin, we rented it, camping out inside for long weekends. It was our second trip to the cabin during winter when we arrived after dark and began getting organized to cook dinner, light a fire, you know, the basic comforts.

We had purchased a folding steel panel to set against the hearth opening between the face of the hearth stones and the fire screen. Its purpose was specifically to keep creatures from coming into the cabin through the chimney while we were not around and to slow the loss of heat when we put the fire to bed for the evening..

I pulled aside the log that braced the screen that braced the panel and peered inside. And closed it back.

I turned to Taylor, who was standing beside me to help light the fire and said, "We have a visitor."

I called Cameron and Beth to come into the den.

"What? What is it?"

"We have a screech owl in the fireplace."

Taylor opened the panel as I reached in with gloved hands to try to catch the owl. All seemed well until the owl scooted through my legs, ending up under the rocking chair behind me. I turned and tried to reach under the chair quickly before it got away. Too late.

In a single transparent motion, the owl lifted into the air and flew into the kitchen. There it fluttered against the window over the sink, searching for an exit, then released a malodorous "comment" in flight which, we are thankful, landed squirt in the sink. As the owl settled into the sink and froze, I wrapped my hands gently around its wings and picked it up.

He was terribly cute and rather big for a screech owl (though still small). His talons (which always seem large for so small a bird) hung limply below my clenched fist, and his eyes stared in a not-so-convincing imitation of a death stare. We took him out onto the back porch, and I set him on a shelf. He did not move. In fact, to maintain his motionless posture, he stood only on the leg on which I set him; the other leg hung through a gap in the shelving. And still he did not move, or even appear to breathe.

We stepped back and enjoyed being able to examine a wild raptor so closely. The kids have seen captured birds (usually with permanent injuries that prevent release back into the wild), but only once before a wild owl up close.

After a few minutes, with no sound or warning, the owl turned and lifted silently into the night, flying up the ridge into the woods. We all marveled at the total absence of sound when he flew. I was close enough to feel the downdraft of his first wing beat, but heard absolutely nothing. Not even a breath of a whisper. It was as if his flight absorbed sound. Magnificent!

This was precisely the type of wildlife encounter we had hoped to have at the cabin. We felt privileged that we had an owl so early in our visiting. In reference to the "comment" deposited into the sink, the kids called it a "present." We still laugh about it.

Soon after moving into the cabin permanently, I was sitting in a chair under the walnut tree, drinking a glass of wine after dinner, when Beth called me into the cabin just after dusk.

"Have you seen this?" She pointed toward the fireplace. Coiled on top of the fire grate was a brand new -- still soft and supple -- and very long snake skin. Easily six feet long. Black snake.

"Did you put that in there?" Beth accused me hopefully.

"Nope. Good thing it's a black snake though." I was searching for something positive and reassuring to say about the fact that we had discovered *inside* the cabin a skin as big as any snake we had seen *outside* the cabin. I did not want to elaborate since I knew what we were all thinking: if it left a fresh skin in the fireplace, where did it come from and, more importantly, where had it gone?

"Probably crawled through a crack higher up the chimney and the skin just fell." I speculated.

No, I didn't believe it, nor did Beth. But maybe the kids did. I went back outside praying that a six foot long black snake would not crawl out from under the sofa while our parents were visiting. Like the mouse did once.

The mouse story happened over Easter weekend when we were still pretty much camping out in the cabin with no furniture except for a breakfast table and a couple of rocking chairs.

We were sleeping on an inflatable mattress in front of the fireplace. Beth woke me in the middle of the night. "I think Nick [our cat] caught a mouse. I can hear it squeaking."

"That's what Nick is supposed to do," I replied and turned over to go back to sleep. The last thing I wanted to do just then was to chase a cat and mouse around the house in the dark of a cold winter night.

"You HAVE to go check!" she pleaded. Her mother was asleep in the kids' room. The kids were in the family room by the fireplace beside us.

I rolled out of my cozy sleeping bag, struggled to stand up and edged over to the door of the kitchen. Nick came prancing toward me out of the shadows created by the nightlight, his mouth full of mouse, tail dangling by his chin.

"Yep, he caught one," I declared.

"Well, get him out!" Beth urged (commanded). I obeyed as best I could.

I opened the back door and directed Nick to exit that way. Like all cats (and unlike dutiful husbands), he ignored my command. Instead, he dropped the mouse so he could pounce on it again. Which he did. Then took a few steps and dropped it, swatted with a front paw and LOST IT. The mouse made a break for the kids' room by way of scooting under a closet door.

"Gone. The mouse got away." I narrated the action to Beth.

"What do you mean 'got away'?"

"He slipped down a crack along the wall, I think." I replied, trying to stretch the truth without abusing it. But I did not want Beth to know that the mouse disappeared in the direction of the kids' room because that was where her mother was sleeping, also on a close-to-the-floor inflatable mattress.

We went back to sleep, or at least I did. The kids

never woke, and Beth slept with the proverbial one eye open.

Next morning, I crawled out of my sleeping bag, lit a fire and settled into my rocking chair with a cup of coffee. Claire, Beth's mother, joined me, rocking in the other chair in front of the fire. Nick wandered over and sat beside Claire's feet and looked at the wood pile.

"That cat acts like it thinks there's a mouse in there," she commented.

I said nothing, but prayed that the stupid mouse would stay where it was, particularly if it was hiding in the wood pile.

"He really seems to think that something is in there, doesn't he?" She queried.

Knowing it would be impolite to ignore her, I replied, "Nah, Nick just wishes there was something for him to chase." I thought about the middle of the night action but did not think the time was right to tell the tale.

Beth stirred in her sleeping bag just behind her mother's rocking chair. "What are you talking about?"

Claire responded, "Look at Nick. He hears or smells something in the woodpile."

Beth and I looked at each other, but I was going to let her break the news to her mom.

Suddenly, Claire shrieked, "A mouse! A mouse!" And she jumped out of the rocking chair.

The mouse ran over Claire's foot, then shot across the hearth in front of me. Nick cut him off to my left, so the mouse leapt into the fireplace where the fire was raging red hot. For an instant, I considered trapping him there where we would be rid of him by virtue of roasting. My humanity prevailed. The mouse escaped the fireplace.

All the shrieking and excitement woke our son and daughter who proceeded to scream with laughter as they watched Nick and me and the mouse all running about the family room. I tried to corral the mouse. Nick tried to catch-and-play. The mouse dashed from wall to wall to hearth and just hoped to live through the next few minutes.

There was a pause in the action when all of us, including Nick, lost track of the mouse. Nick kept searching around the left side of the hearth, but could not locate the mouse.

Then Beth spied the fury little varmint sitting about two feet up on a small ledge of protruding rock that formed part of the hearth. The mouse could not have been twelve inches from Nick's nose. As Beth pointed to him, Nick saw the mouse at last and swatted. The mouse jumped from the ledge to the floor and spun around neatly to slip through the crack at the back of the hearth. Gone.

Everyone was safe at last.

Fortunately for me, Claire was a good sport, and

patient. She lived on the side of a mountain ridge near West Jefferson in northwestern North Carolina and had her own family of mice that enjoyed her basement in winter. So, she understood, sort of.

****

In the hill house, which was built into the hillside just beyond the back door, there was a square bag of loose insulation like the kind you blow into attics. It was unopened when first we discovered it in early winter. A month later, I stopped by to check on things and opened the hill house door. I noticed a pile of what appeared to be gray dust in a small pile beside the bag. Then I heard a rustling that seemed to come from within the bag. A small nose, followed by whiskers on a small gray face appeared, looked up at me, then disappeared, emerging a few moments later to climb the wall and exit just below the eaves.

A second later, the entire scene was repeated as another mouse departed the bag.

Those two gave Cameron much joy as he kept opening the hill house each time we visited in hopes of seeing the mice. Naturally, as a four year old, he always reported that he had been successful and had seen the mice. Being parents, we were skeptical until, after several sorties to see the mice, Cameron yelled from the spring house, "I saw it! I saw the mouse!" Then we knew it was real by the excitement and surprise in his voice.

The first few times that I mowed the pasture, I came across box turtles. The first was a small one about three to four inches in length. The next was a normal size adult who retreated into his shell and would not come out no matter how long the kids played with him or waited for him to emerge from his shell inside the cardboard box home they built for the turtle. He was ultimately so docile, if not to say boring, that the kids named him Pokey. After a few hours of trying to see him do something, anything, we released him and have not seen him again.

The next adult box turtle I saw took great interest in the noise and blade wash from the lawn tractor (manly tool). A very curious turtle, he extended his neck full length to investigate the source of noise and vibration. When the kids arrived to investigate the turtle, he beat a rapid retreat in the direction of the creek. A mere twenty-five feet away, he might have made it if the kids had not cut off his escape route. They watched him and he them for fifteen minutes or so all the while maneuvering around each other; the turtle trying to charge to the creek, the kids being sure that he did not leave before they had had their fun watching him and exploring his jaws and claws. This turtle far surpassed the previous; they named him Swifty and dabbed a dot of red fingernail polish on his shell to identify him later. Later happened to be the next time I mowed the lower pasture, so they all enjoyed another session.

Cameron asked one day if we could explore the creek under the "bridge", which is actually the corrugated steel culvert over which our driveway crosses the creek. He and I got our rubber boots on and climbed down the bank of the creek and waded along the edge up to the culvert. Inside the culvert, the noise of the creek was amplified and Cameron shrieked for effect to hear the echo. As I stood near the upstream edge of the pipe, I saw something drift past my boot. It looked like a dead crawfish so I picked it up to show it to Cameron.

It was alive and turned out to be a small lobster, the biggest crawfish I had ever seen.

"Look Cameron, a crawdad, or crawfish."

Cameron looked at the squirming crustacean between my fingers, the claws swinging wildly in an attempt to pinch me.

"What did you say it was?" Cameron asked me.

"Well, I said crawdad, but…"

Cameron interrupted me, "Are there crawkids?"

When I stopped laughing, I said "Yes, of course

there are crawkids."

After that, along with various sizes of salamanders, Cameron was the champion finder of crawkids.

Our children's experiences with both flora and fauna that they did not see in Atlanta was obviously one of the best things about living at the cabin. Whether mice, snakes (outside), turtles, hawks, owls, salamanders or crawfish in the creek, or rabbits in the pastures; all of us are savored seeing and watching the wildlife.

Everyone became braver and more comfortable about co-existing with the local animals and insects.

****

One night, Beth and I were catching the late night news in the loft just before going to sleep. As I turned out my reading light, a flutter of small wings passed overhead.

"What was that?!" Beth inquired, not quite at ease.

"Has to be a bat," I replied matter-of-factly. One must stay cool in the face of panic.

A few more low overhead passes and Nick snatched the bat from the air. We heard the angry and fearful squeaking as Nick probably "tasted" his prey. Then the bat flew again. [Remember the mouse; we knew that Nick would not simply capture and terminate the bat.]

Back and forth under the angled roofline of the loft. Beth ducked under the covers, fearing a bat nest in her hair. I began to laugh. Somewhat insensitive I know. But it was just too funny that we had had so many interesting encounters in the short time that we had lived here.

"Where is it?" Beth's muffled voice peeked from under the quilt.

"On the wall now. I just have to think how to

catch him. Woops!" I ducked as the bat again took flight, to and fro. Nick caught him again and, again, released him. He returned to a quiet perch on the north wall of the loft above the small windows, the highest, darkest spot.

I found a nearby shoe box, removed the shoes (Beth's, and she did not know it at the time because she was still under the covers) and tore one end of the top. I quickly placed the box over the bat, and it immediately expressed its displeasure by squeaking and flapping around inside the box. I slipped the top against the wall and eased it upward between the box and the wall, careful not to leave too large an escape at the bottom of the box, until it covered the opening of the box.

"Got it." I declared, thankful for small victories.

I went out onto the front porch, stepped into the night and released our little friend.

"How do you think he got in?" Beth asked when I returned to the loft.

"No idea. Probably came in through the chimney."

That became my pat answer for anything inside that should have been outside.

****

Our first autumn, Cameron was sitting in a chair to the side of the fireplace. He looked over to where Beth and I were sitting on the sofa and said very casually, "I just saw a pair of eyes." He gestured toward where the fireplace separated from the logs when we had the rear wall of the cabin raised. "Big round eyes. But I don't know what it is. It doesn't look like a mouse."

I interrogated him to be sure he was not hallucinating or having religiously induced visions. Satisfied that it was, at most, nothing more than a child's imagination, we continued with our conversation and thought nothing more of it.

We had adopted a new cat, Harley, who had a

bad habit of jumping onto any surface that intrigued him and worrying not a whit that he knocked breakable items to the floor. Because he was still young and pretty demanding, even for a cat, we endured the antics; of course, because he was a cat, we knew we had no choice, cats being perfectly untrainable.

During the winter, I liked to wake between three and five AM to put another log on the fire. Unfortunately, when I woke, I could rarely return to sleep, so I used it as a quiet time for uninterrupted reading. After an hour or so, I usually put down my book and rediscovered the pleasant world behind my eyelids until dawn.

One night, I had returned to my ethereal world of peace and rest when I heard something fall. "Harley!" I accused and threw a cloth napkin in his direction.

Harley stopped in his tracks but would not move. Then Nick, our number one cat, crept up to the hearth and froze, looking upward. I flipped on my book light and saw a small creature doing anti-gravity moves along the face of the fireplace and the underside of the mantel. I jumped up and turned on the lights.

Two large beady black eyes peered from a gap between the fireplace and the hearth. Thinking it was a mouse, I stepped to the front door and unlocked it so that the cats could chase it outside when it ran. It held its ground below the mantel, so I slipped closer and found that it was larger than a mouse. And longer. Not a rat, thank goodness, but neither was it a squirrel. Or rather, it was not a common gray squirrel.

A flying squirrel!? Both question and recognition. We had not seen flying squirrels around the property nor had I ever seen one in person before. But sure enough, that was what it was.

The cats stretched and paced and peered and tried to find a way to snatch the squirrel from its perch.

Then it was gone, vanished through the big crack between the fireplace hearth stones and the logs of the cabin wall, disappeared right where Cameron had seen his "big round eyed" creature some weeks before.

When Beth woke, I assured her that it had departed the same way it had come, through a crack behind the fireplace. As had become customary, I hoped the story I made up was pretty close to the truth.

*****

It was the middle of a long winter night, and all the cabin was asleep, all except for the small creatures scratching, gamboling, dashing and sliding above my head.

Beth and I had our bedroom in the loft above the family room. The ceiling followed the roofline as it sloped upward, then flattened across the center of the space creating a small "attic". There was no access to the attic space; that is, there was no access for us.

The first winter in the cabin, we had a family of squirrels that resided, conceived and raised a family in the wall at the head of our bed, the dead air space between the inside wall and the outside wall. The furry creatures were noisy at wee hours when we would have preferred to have been sleeping, but it was cute – well, maybe novel is a better word – to host a family of squirrels for the winter.

As cute as it was, I was supposed to block the hole beside the top of the stone chimney by which they gained entry. Unfortunately, the hole was just out of reach of my longest ladder. But then, the next year was not the year that they wanted to live in that wall.

Nevertheless, with the arrival of the first really cold nights, we heard small footsteps overhead and thought that the mice that seem to live everywhere on the property – hill house, garage, barn, shed -- had decided to also live in the "attic". Beth and I talked about the joys of mice versus squirrels and concluded that we preferred the mice. They were smaller and thus quieter. Good theory, and perhaps even accurate so far as it was true.

The farther the temperature dropped, the louder our attic friends became. Soon, it sounded as if an entire colony had settled in for holiday festivities. The early part of the night was generally peaceful with a few small rustling sounds. But sometimes there was the sound of excited running with quick turns and dashes that must have been a game of tag. And always, just before dawn, the crescendo of little claws tapping as the critters awoke. That was often followed by the sound of sliding, one by one, down the inside of the ceiling below the roof.

Several years previous, when we lived in Atlanta, we had a "mouse" problem. Sitting in the den, we could hear them partying away in the walls. When we visited the basement, we heard a herd of them scurrying to wherever surprised mice scurry. It was almost Christmas, and Beth was pregnant. So, she was frequently awake and sitting in the den in the middle of the night hearing scratching so loud she knew that the mice were coming through the wall any minute. We called the exterminator and he placed poison bait, but confided in me that we did not seem to have a mouse problem. I assured Beth that all was fine, but secretly began to wonder.

I visited the basement more frequently and especially every time we heard noises from down below. After a few visits, I learned the pattern of the scurrying. I also noticed the noise of mouse feet over suspended ceiling tiles was much louder than I expected.

Following the path of the invaders one evening, I watched as they dropped from the ceiling into an open closet and ran across the top of a bookcase to disappear through a gap in the wall that passed into the crawlspace under the house. Finally, I knew the truth. Rats!

I called the exterminator again. He came while I was at work and told my wife that he was putting out rat bait. Beth called me at my office. "Guess what? We've got rats." I replied, "Yes, I know; I didn't want to tell you because I knew you would just worry."

With that kind of history behind us, Beth immediately suspected that I was being less than forthright about our cabin guests. "They're rats, aren't they?" "No. I promise. Rats would be much louder." She pretended to believe me.

I did not mention how relieved I was that we never heard the sound of a large black snake slithering above the ceiling as they have been known to do.

THE CATS

When we lived in Atlanta, we had an old cat, a fluffy bundle of calico named Tasha, who had been declawed by a previous owner. Despite having no front claws, she hunted squirrels, chipmunks and sometimes a small rabbit; she was particularly adept at catching chipmunks. She loved being outside and suffered few humans; she would occasionally acquiesce to affection for us, but that was usually associated with belly rubs or a special meal of fish or chicken parts. She disappeared one fall, and we knew that she had left to die.

Basically, we are dog people but have enjoyed one cat at a time. On the other hand we had three dogs at the same time, all black Labradors. The dogs were older than our children and got along well with everyone, including our cat.

Our next cat was a skinny gray tabby kitten named Jasmine. She was none too bright but very loving and playful. The dogs endured her kittenish hyperactivity at a time when two of the three wanted to spend most of their day snoozing in the middle of the den floor. Before Jasmine was a year old, the cat next door came over and picked a fight. Jasmine got infected (literally "cat scratch fever") and died suddenly.

A few months after Jasmine's death, another neighbor knew we were down to one old Labrador, Ranger, aged 14, and called to see if we would give a home to a cat from the Animal Shelter. His owner, an elderly widow, had passed away and Frog needed a home. Our neighbor made us promise that the cat would be kept indoors; we said that was fine. If the cat likes being indoors, we certainly are not going to make it go outside. She clarified that we must *prevent* at all costs the escape of the cat because "it could get killed or worse since it knows nothing about being outside." We did not really know what to expect and were not especially enthused about having to have cat litter in our utility room for an indoor cat, but we agreed to accept the cat. We should have known better than to become involved in someone else's pet rules.

Frog came to live with us. I half expected a green tabby or chartreuse calico or something out of Dr. Seuss, but he was perfectly, radiantly pitch black. He had one flop ear filled with stitches from a bad fight at the Animal Shelter. Still, he was gentle and easy going. He walked right up to Ranger and stuck his face on Ranger's nose. Ranger responded casually by snapping his mouth onto Frog's head. No damage, just a friendly declaration of Ranger's supremacy in the household.

We did not understand why an elderly woman would name a cat Frog. But then he walked up to the water bowl and sniffed before stepping into it with his two front paws. He always drank that way. Sometimes he swatted at the water as if trying to break the smooth reflection of his image in the bowl.

The first thing we did, since we could not let him outside, was change his name. It was easy for me to change his name because I do not think that cats know their names (and know cat lovers who will vehemently challenge this prejudice). It was just before Christmas, so our children thought we should name the cat Santa Claus. We explained that Santa Claus was a difficult name to share and they eventually accepted Nick -- for St. Nicholas.

Nick seemed relieved to have a new home, relieved for his release from the purgatory of the Animal Shelter and settled into our house. He never even looked at a door much less tried to go outside. It was all just as we had been told.

As the season warmed into spring, Nick periodically shot out the sliding glass door onto the deck. Once there, he seemed confused about what the next step should be. We would catch him easily and quickly return him to the cloistered safety of indoors. It seemed a game for him, a game that included being captured quickly and willingly. For a while.

Then came the day that he shot out the door, dashed across the deck and bolted over the grass to the back of the yard where he scrambled up the gnarly bark of an old twisted pine. Stopping, he looked around, surprised he had made it. No one had caught him. No one tried to follow him up the tree. Our daughter was calling him from the deck, but he could ignore that easily enough, and he did.

All went well. A little game we played. Nick escaped every now and then. We returned him to the house and admonished him to behave like the indoor cat we had been told he had to be. We lost more and more matches. Nick spent longer and longer outside. The neighbor who had arranged the adoption scolded us, reminding us of our promise to keep him inside. I tried to explain that we were not encouraging him to go outside; he took it upon himself, and he enjoyed it. She scowled.

Then we moved to the cabin.

Nick hated traveling in a car. Whenever he traveled by car, he always made a point of throwing up within the first ten minutes. Sometimes he did worse. We took him to the cabin with us for a Christmas visit and then a New Year's vacation. He prowled the land and the woods. No doubt he sniffed the scent of mice and moles, possum, raccoon and rabbit. He was quite content patrolling the front porch and equally content to nestle by the fire when long cold winter evenings stilled the cove.

He looked like someone who had found home after a long sojourn.

When we visited for Easter, Nick disappeared. When it was time for us to drive back to Atlanta, he was nowhere to be found. Because he was a cat, I was certain that he knew we were calling and searching for him, but he stayed hidden. I suspected that he was hiding under the cabin where it was too dark for me to find him even with a flashlight. But he may have been off in the woods up on the ridge for all I know.

After an hour of looking for him, we had no choice. We piled his bowl on the back porch bench high with food and left. I had to come back in a few days to check on our contractor, so we hoped I could get him then.

I did. As I pulled into the drive, I saw Nick leaning over the creek, drinking water like a dog, and I knew then that he was very independent; he was okay.

We moved furniture into the cabin a week before we moved ourselves. I drove the truck up. Beth and the kids came with odds and ends and the cat. Nick was so pleased to be back in the mountains that we all agreed he could probably make it a few days without us and saved him another round trip in the car.

Like any cat who is allowed outdoors, Nick

stalked all manner of wildlife from crickets and granddaddy longlegs to birds. He irritated me in a pleasant way by going out the back screen door – well, really *through* the door since our dog, Scout (then an always-tumbling-over, rubbery puppy), broke the screen loose. Soon Nick would come around to the front door and meow to get in. This went on most of the day, except when he crawled into a dark corner of the loft to sleep.

I thought the in-and-out routine was pretty funny for a while, but then he seemed to be constantly asking to be out when he was in and in when he was out. Someone always seemed to be thinking that he had been where he was for long enough that he needed to change location. Doors opened and closed and opened and closed. Nick was in then out then out then in.

After a few months of this, I became dizzy and almost nauseous with the frequency of his changing locations. I no longer believed that even a cat could be so energetic about where he wanted to be because he never stayed where he was long enough to need to move.

It all came to a head when I let him in the back door one afternoon as I was going outside to light the stone grill. Nick went in as I went out. I lit the kindling to start the fire in the grill and then went back inside by way of the front door. As I crossed the den, I saw Nick sitting on the back porch eating from his bowl on the bench. No one had entered or left the cabin since I went out to light the fire. Moreover, if someone had opened the back door, I would have heard it and seen them since the grill is only about thirty unobstructed feet from the back porch.

I called to Beth and asked if she knew where Nick was. She said he was in the kids' room with her.

But I could see a black cat eating at Nick's bowl on the back porch.

Another black cat. Same size and shape. Indistinguishable.

We named him Ditto.

We had no idea whether Ditto was a he or a she. I referred to him in the masculine because Nick was male and I did not want to become any more confused than necessary when identifying to two identical black cats. But he, Ditto, could very easily have been female.

Ditto never let us near him.

During the early days, Ditto ran whenever he heard us or saw us standing at the window watching him. We were still trying to see in what ways he could be distinguished from Nick; a little thinner in the face, eyes a brighter green and no ear flop.

Ditto talked a lot. We saw him trotting across the yard from the tractor barn to the woods, making a noise that was more like a bark than a meow. He seemed full of himself, chatting noisily, glancing about for Nick, heading for his ridge-side lair. A dandy fellow, we hoped that he might become part of the family.

One evening, I was grilling and noticed that

Ditto had perched on the back porch bench, eating "Nick's" food (we had been leaving plenty of food for both cats for months). The back door was open, though the screen door was closed as usual; however, the screen door remained torn. Then I noticed that Ditto was not eating on the bench. I wondered.

I stepped over to the porch, eased up the steps and peered into the kitchen. I called to Beth and she answered from the loft where she and the kids were gathering laundry. Then I saw a black cat emerge from the kids' room. Ditto. He stopped, looked at me blocking the doorway and then sped along the wall, scanning for an exit. I opened the screen door and he shot past me.

I really thought that might have signaled his final hurdle to accepting us as a home for him. But summer seized all of us in its grip of heat and heavy air, and Ditto decided that outdoors was where he wished to be. With plenty of critters to hunt, he stopped by only occasionally for a snack -- and often that was in the middle of the night, tripping the motion-activated light over the back porch.

You never know how a pet will react to a new animal in the house. Nick could be tough (he had chased a German Shepherd off our land), so we thought he would be territorial when it came to Ditto. In fact, we had previously considered adopting other cats to help with mice or snakes around the barn and such, but had acknowledged that those cats would have to be forever outdoor cats in deference to Nick (it is a small cabin). Therefore, we were surprised when one day Beth spied Nick on the back porch, leaning over to rub heads and whiskers with Ditto, who was seated on the step below Nick. The two cats seemed affectionate in the way you would expect of loving siblings.

While it is in our nature to want to possess in some way those things that we like, we really had the best of everything with Ditto. We had a wild animal that was not wild and a pet that was not a pet. He liked visiting and we liked his visits. But we did not possess him nor he us. He lived his life as we did ours, each enjoying the periodic intersection with the other.

****

A couple years later, after one of our son's soccer games, we stopped at a new burrito cafe for lunch. As we left, we saw a window filled with cats. Big cats. One all white, another all black and some gray and calico in between. There was a sign that read HOME NEEDED.

We returned the following week and talked to the people who ran the Cat Clinic. The all-white cat was named Moose, and he was deaf. The only cat that really needed a home of all the huge cats in the window was the all black cat named Harley. The staff let me and the kids into the cat room and the kids settled onto the floor to play with Harley.

Now, ostensibly, this visit in the cat room was for the purpose of determining *whether* we liked the cat enough to take it home with us. As you can imagine, the farce was pretending that there was a decision to be made. I left the room for a private inquiry about the rules and business of adopting the cat, its incurable and contagious diseases as well as its propensity for inflicting serious physical injury. The responses were not all perfect, but there seemed no reason on which I could hang a parent's refusal to add another pet to the family. So, we borrowed a cat crate and tossed it with the cat into the back seat of my car and sped home.

When we piled out of the car at the cabin, Beth acted surprised that we had adopted the cat.

Harley fit his name. Although just two years old when we adopted him, he was a big cat with powerful forelegs, long hair, mane and a leonine face. In short, he was a miniature of the big African cats. He lounged on the arm of our armchair as if resting on the limb of a tree in the heat of a Tsavo summer day.

He was also asthmatic, wheezing softly as he slept curled on the quilt on our bed. He frequently had a runny nose.

Nick was unfriendly to Harley at first. Then he feigned friendship to lure Harley within nosing range, at which point Nick would spit and hiss, popping Harley with his paws. Harley, in turn, did the same to Scout. Scout, the innocent puppy (and youngest of our pets), looked dazed and bemused at this new Nick with a different smell and a bad attitude.

All in all, Harley was a bit of a street punk. He constantly annoyed us to let him out. As soon as he was out, he began scratching the window pane to get in. Or he banged the screen door. Or stood at the back door and pulled himself up high enough to look into the window, all the while meowing as if his life might suddenly end if we did not drop everything and respond. He refused to let us hold him, but if I was talking on the phone outside, he would curl up against my back while I sat on the picnic table. No matter how many times I stood or moved, he resettled into the same position. If I tried to scratch his head, he pulled away. If I was reading or tying flies, Harley begged incessantly for a scratch.

Nick was a great sleeping companion. He nestled behind our knees and adjusted without complaint when we rolled over. Harley collapsed on top of our legs and would not move no matter how difficult it may have been for us to sleep in a given position. Both cats were determined to wake us when they were ready to rise in the morning without regard to whether the sun had yet risen. Harley also banged the front window with a great rattling noise until we woke and let him in or out, whichever he was not.

Neither cat responded to the noise of flying squirrels in the attic space over our bedroom loft (although both got very interested in *watching* when a flying squirrel appeared on the hearth as written previously). Ridding our world of rodent pests would have made the cats useful; but no doubt they would have lost their Cat Union card that guarantees all cats the right to sleep, be fed, disdain their owners and generally laze through life.

****

A few months after adopting Harley, he did not report for breakfast. Until that day, he had never missed a meal.

Beth found him in our side yard seriously injured. He had been hit by a car. She could not tell how extensive the injuries, but it was clear he had severe lacerations on one leg, likely broken bones in at least two others. Beth took him immediately to the emergency vet.

Harley's tongue was almost completely severed. The vet told Beth that cats cannot survive without their tongues and while surgery was an option, there was a good chance it would not succeed. This made the broken hip (in two places) and broken foreleg seem unimportant.

Surgery or no? It would be very expensive with no assurance that he would live. Even if he lived, a failed surgery to reattach the tongue would mean that we would have to put him to sleep. If successful, it would be a rough recovery requiring that Harley live in a dog crate and be hand-fed (food and water) through a syringe for several weeks.

Was it truly worth putting all of us through trying to save this cat? Was it worth the hope and potential disappointment?

Beth and I have long joked about how much money our "free" animals have cost us. It always seems to be more than the ones we paid for. Here it was again.

The closest that Harley could have been when hit by the car was one hundred fifty feet. Only one leg was not completely disabled in the accident. Yet, he managed to pull himself all the way back to the cabin yard where he waited for help.

Courage, loyalty, love. I did not know which of these drove Harley, or whether it was some mix of all, or whether it was base survival instinct. I chose to believe that he knew we would help him because we loved him. He wanted to survive. We could not abandon him to fate. We had to try to save him.

The surgery on Harley's tongue did not work, but Harley adapted. His recovery was every bit as hard as the vet said it would be, and our children were excellent caregivers, feeding Harley liquid food through a syringe for weeks.

Sadly, a few months later, Nick was also hit by a car. By the time we found him at a neighbor's house, he had suffered too long to survive. We buried him on the ridge behind the cabin.

****

Several months after Nick's death, Beth was driving down a remote road on her way back from the Nature Center when she spied a small kitten on the side of the road. It was raining and there were no houses in sight, so she knew that she had to rescue it. Our children named it Little Bit.

Little Bit could fit in my palm. She (or he, it was too young to tell) was an adorable tabby. She survived only four days; the dehydration had taken too great a toll.

Little Bit died in her sleep Saturday night. After we lost her, all of us felt an emptiness. It was not deep like when you lose a family member or a close friend who has filled many good days of your life. But it was a similar emptiness, one marked by the loss of hope, a hope based on the expectation of many happy days and hours of tenderness and love. Little Bit had been almost a pound of promise and hope. She was gone, likely lost before Beth and the children ever found her wet, hungry, dehydrated and lonely on the side of a desolate road.

When Beth and our children had been in the vet's office having Little Bit checked and medicated, the assistant at the desk had asked if they did not have room for one or three more kittens at home. She was keeping three orphans and needed to find a home for them. One needy waif of a kitten seemed enough, especially when we realized how it would disrupt Harley's world as the cat at the center of our universe.

Two days after Little Bit died, Beth called the vet to see if the kittens still needed a home. Two of them did. We agreed that we should bring both home with us. Harley was not likely to befriend a kitten, and the two kittens would have each other.

We named the female calico Soleil. We named the male tabby Moony (though I called him Moonman). Two months later, we called both of them Hooligans.

Soleil was a prissy calico whose spine hair seemed always primped and vertical. Her eyes were masked by swatches of black, making it impossible to tell from a distance if she was awake and watching or sound asleep. Her nose was clownish with a similar patch of black making her look a bit like a scarecrow. She was the more vocal of the two, meowing loudly at anything or nothing, including her need to use the litter box.

Moony was a stout gray tabby with a swath of white running from his face down his belly and onto his paws. His fur was dense, but his tail striping was faint and visible only in bright light. He was energetic, but rarely the aggressor. When "attacked" by Soleil, he always landed on top, from which she had trouble flipping him. He was a cat's cat, generally aloof. Moony could barely manage a squeak of a meow.

Acrobatic balls of fire and fur. Pin sharp teeth and prickly claws. No windowsill or table top or upholstery was safe when they were awake. Fearless and tireless until they collapsed, suddenly and completely, after a couple of hours of non-stop chasing, climbing, fighting, sparring, stalking and pouncing.

The kittens kept a fairly regular schedule of eating, followed by a couple of hours of play, followed by more eating and an hour or so of play. On and on, with the periods of play declining and the periods of rest increasing. Unfortunately, they did not keep their schedules according to a clock.

I awoke one morning about 3:00 AM. I went into the den and grabbed a book, my glasses and a headlamp by which to read. The kittens heard me and came tumbling down the steps from the loft. I kept quiet, hoping they would do the same. They poked around a bit, seeming sleepy. But then they began to spar, and run, and climb, and topple anything they could topple.

I continued to read, trying to ignore them into silence.

After an hour of noisy play, I decided I might try to "teach" them how to stop and go to sleep in their bed. I intended to pick each of them up and place them in their bed, thereby suggesting that it was time to sleep. Not really thinking how I must look to them with a headlight beaming from my otherwise invisible-in-the-dark face, I picked up Moony. He screamed and bit solidly into my index finger. Not a quick bite-and-release, but a solid, I am going to hold you until I die kind of bite. Unable to reason with him, I instinctively flung him from his death grip on my finger. He landed hard on the floor and howled even louder. Although I could not imagine how he could hurt worse than I did, I knelt to console him. He howled even louder, as if he were being tortured to death slowly.

It hit me as fast as any thought comes to me when I am awake in the pre-dawn morning-- all Moony could see was the headlamp. He did not know it was me. He saw only a terrible and invisible creature, a dark giant, able to seize a poor kitten from play and toss it to the floor, capable of squeezing the very life from the defenseless (in Moony's mind) kitten.

On the other hand, it was I who was bleeding profusely from a bite that went to the bone.

In the morning, I woke with a nasty looking finger, blood red at the knuckle and a dark spot at the site of the puncture. Moony ambled into the kitchen and rubbed against my leg as if it had all been a bad dream. For me.

All three of our cats provided endless entertainment. They were loving, but detached as cats are. They were clever hunters, but often pretended they could not find the food bowl on the back porch. They were demanding, but we loved them.

FLORA

I mentioned previously that there were seasons for the wildlife, especially insects. There were seasons for the flora also. First the dogwoods bloom in spring, close on the heels of a passing winter, their spray of white blossoms scattered through the woods as if painted by Monet. Soon after, the wildflowers would emerge.

Trilliums. The first we spotted was a small and discrete Nodding Trillium nestled among the ferns just above the moss-edged creek. Then we noticed another plant with large mottled leaves like the Nodding Trillium, with a deep purple in its petals and a maroon stamen trimmed in gold; Toadshade (red trillium). Then, a glorious yellow flower with small blood red stamens; Trout Lily (erythronium umbilicatum).

Jack-in-the-pulpit, with its slightly obscene (phallic) purple spadix rising below the striped and folded "pulpit"; Cameron loved that one best of all, calling it "jack in the bulbit". They grew mostly along the creek bank with some plants reaching over three feet in height.

One day, searching in the woods for a fallen white pine, Cameron and I stumbled across a small patch of delicate bulbs, so pink and soft they appeared a surreal sort of flesh: Pink Lady's Slipper.

Asters, violets, touch-me-nots. More "common" flowers than I could identify or remember. Flowers at once wild and beautiful, anything but common, weeds by any other name. And finally the prolific Cherokee primrose (a thorn by any other name: briars) as the heat of summer overcame the cool spring days and nights.

In the woods, after the dogwoods, rhododendron, mountain laurel and wild flame azalea, a surprising and stunning orange.

With autumn, another wave of wildflowers bloomed. Small purple flowers of a wild and shrubby locust. Orange and red spotted Touch-me-nots along the roadside, often growing in close proximity to poison ivy for which it is an antidote. The roadside embankments were filled with color that we should have stopped to enjoy and identify more regularly.

Forest, woods, groves and coves. Everything from a few well-placed pines (yellow and white) to fallen chestnuts, casualties of the blight, to the protected cove of virgin poplar in Joyce Kilmer Memorial Forest south of Slickrock Wilderness, a place long special to me. Oak, hemlock, maple.

We know the value of mature trees. They are irreplaceable. Simply and absolutely irreplaceable. Although wood is a renewable resource and should be valued as such when considering timber, it is not truly a renewable resource when considering the esthetics of woods or forests. During our years at the cabin, I turned fifty. The number of the age did not bother me so much, but one of the implications did. I would never see a tree I planted fully mature in my life time. (I did not plant ornamentals that might mature in that time period, only native trees that would not.)

Sure, you can buy trees for planting and replanting. You can even buy large trees that cost a fortune to install; I say install because it is more of a construction project than planting process. But you cannot buy a mature fifty foot oak. Or a mature seventy foot hemlock. Or any number of large tree species that need a variety of favorable factors, mostly time, to grow to full maturity.

Notwithstanding the so-called "fast growth" hybrids of pine, a good tree, a natural tree, takes many years, usually decades, to reach maturity. And those years are fraught with severe weather, disease, and human action. Ice storms, strong winds, tornados, insects and parasites, development and, in some ways worst of all because often it can be avoided, fire.

We have already had a few incidents of high wind taking a toll: three large white pines, the smallest of which was easily sixty feet tall. In each case, the tree had a major branching of the trunk that must have created a weakness where, in winds gusting over fifty miles per hour, the trunk split, dropping a half or more of the tree to the ground. I cringed whenever I woke to the roar of wind rushing across the ridge above us; I knew that trees would fall and I hated to lose another large, old growth hemlock or white pine.

From a distance, the ridge above the cove was spotted with patches of brown where pine beetles had killed their namesake trees, especially the yellow pines. Having devastated the adjoining stands, the hungry beetles began finding our trees. Solution per the expert we consulted? Cut the yellow pine trees and a one hundred foot buffer to minimize the spread, not necessarily defeat it.

Sell the timber? I wished. Because of the drought and the pine beetles (somewhat inter-related as the drought weakens the trees' resistance to beetles and disease), the market was flooded with yellow pine cut to stop the spread of the pestilence. Moreover, there was a good chance that the beetles might have also enabled blue stain, a fungus that discolored the wood, rendering it undesirable for lumber. Best case, if we had been lucky, someone might have cut and removed the timber for no cost to us. But that never happened.

Development left a conspicuous vacancy next door where our neighbors (before we bought our cabin) clear-cut most of their three acres and planted grass up the steep hillside. It was a well-kept yard, but more Southern plantation style than a mountain home. Their clear-cutting had, naturally, spawned erosion, flooding our creek with red mud when the rains were heavy. While I am sure that they did not intend to cause erosion, it seems all too common for environmental damage to be "unintentional".

Early one November, we went up to Mt Mitchell, the highest mountain in the eastern United States, to hike. Driving back home along the Blue Ridge Parkway, Cameron and Beth spotted a plume of smoke in the distance across the valley. None of us could guess what it might be, but it was very distinct. As we approached the last exit before ours, a Park Ranger blocked the way with his car, his lights flashing. We detoured and intersected with the Parkway near our exit, and spotted brown smoke billowing skyward. Forest fire.

Prior to December, we had had only a couple of days of rain over the preceding few months. The woods were tender dry. A statewide burning ban was in effect and had been for a couple of weeks. It turned out that the fire was contained after burning about twenty-five acres. The fire burned on the northwest side of the Swannanoa Mountain, the south side of which was where we lived. The fire was more than two miles as the crow flies, but it caused me to remark that forest fires were never something that we had to worry about in the suburbs of Atlanta.

Five days later, I stepped out of the cabin and inhaled sharply acrid, bitter air that I thought must be downdraft from our own woodstove. I walked into the yard, turned and examined the chimney for slow cold smoke that would be drifting down. Nothing. Then I realized it was smoke from a forest fire many miles away. The dingy pall and sharp, pungent smoke was stifling. The mountains were smothered in a brownish yellow haze. Although there was a breeze, the air itself was stale, harsh and distressing to breathe.

I learned later that the smoke came from a fire in Madison County, more than thirty miles to our north, a fire that had burned 700 acres and was less than twenty percent under control. Five days later, the fire was 95% controlled, but by then it had burned over 2700 acres.

None of the fires became a threat to us. And I had no fear that they would become a threat. Yet, it could have happened. A fire from a neighbor burning trash could ignite the woods, the winds carrying it across the mountainside and down the cove, swept across the ridge face.

Very disturbing were rumors of volunteer firemen starting fires designed to burn toward the national forests. No homes were immediately threatened and the firemen were called for forest fire work for which they were paid. While we all hated to think that a rational person would intentionally set a forest fire, the mountains are a land of independent and, to some degree, self-preservation-oriented mountaineers.

From the earliest days, the mountain people recognized that the rules of government often favored the valley farmer and the city businessman to the detriment of the mountaineer (a term they find somewhat less offensive than hillbilly). Moonshine, blockade, mountain dew, corn. Call it by most any name, for more than a century, it was the only cash crop for many mountain families. Homemade liquor was portable in a way that corn was not. There was no real market for the mountain agriculture because there was no real market. The people grew what they needed to survive and that was the limit of most farms' productivity. Barter worked among the mountain folk, but did not answer the need for occasional cash. Even when a farm produced a bit more than it needed for its own consumption or barter, there was no efficient way to get the crops to market. No trains; only small, rough mountain paths, muddy, rocky and long. Hard for man and beast.

In the same way today, many a hardworking mountain man labors most of his daylight hours for a modest wage in construction or at one of the few remaining mills. He often moonlights. And he hunts for his meat, diligently shooting deer until his and his neighbors' freezers are filled. Then he volunteers himself and his well-worn pickup truck to attend to local fires and other fire department emergencies (car wrecks, etc.), a truly valuable contribution for the community. When the holidays roll around, he, like the rest of us, is eager to make the days special for his family. But he may not have the extra cash on hand after the essentials of food, gas, rent and property taxes. How to find an overtime opportunity when days are shorter and the weather poor? Burn some national forest land so that his fire department will be called to help put it out. He might rationalize that no one gets hurt and the money comes from the federal government, for which he is likely to have little use anyway.

We did not have a lot of land, and we did not value it for its timber so much as its woods. An evergreen grove along the pastures was backed by scattered hardwoods and a laurel thicket up the ridge from the cabin. It was a pleasant and moderately open woods for a walk.

It could all have burned in an hour, maybe less.

Of course, like the woods, the cabin was mostly trees. Whole logs with two sides flattened by an adze. The hundred and fifty year old wood was well seasoned, the kind of timber that burns freely and enthusiastically, the kind of wood I want in the woodstove on a cold night. Oak, pine, chestnut; the cabin was built of the indigenous species most readily available in the mid-nineteenth century.

The evergreen grove was a mix of large white pines, a few exquisite and stately hemlocks and a smattering of short leaf, yellow pines which the pine beetles were decimating all over the ridge. The deciduous hardwoods were represented by oaks of three varieties (red, white and black), sturdy locusts, gnarly black walnuts, elegant dogwoods and magnificent poplars that ripened into gold in the early fall. A few red maples and sycamores along with some wild cherry trees that my landscape architect friend, Harry, called "bullshit" trees.

"Just cut them down. All they do is attract web worms."

Although I did not think Harry felt that way most of the time, it was noteworthy how quickly neighbors and friends would suggest that cutting a tree was a solution to something that was not yet a problem.

A walnut grew beside the septic tank; "better cut that down before the roots get into the septic system."

A dead locust stood near the cabin but too far away to hit anything when it fell; "better cut that tree before an ice storm topples it."

A sick maple spread its limbs beside the garage and, in the front yard, a dying one hundred fifty year old American Holly still produced magnificent, lusciously red berries for Christmas decorating: "better cut them down; they're dying anyway."

No, I liked my trees standing tall, making shade, dancing and sighing in the wind. I even liked them standing as abstract sculpture and animal nesting (woodpeckers, squirrels, owls) after they had died so long as they did not threaten immediate damage or danger.

Just behind the stone grill stood the dead trunk

of an old growth white pine. It was three feet in diameter and rose fifty feet (the top half of the tree had long since toppled into the pasture), wreathed in poison ivy vines as much as four inches thick. I severed the vines, but enjoyed the memorial of the trunk, a reminder of what the forests of these mountains looked like before the timber companies clear cut virtually every acre. Similarly, I knew that when the American Holly in the front yard died, we would trim the ends of the branches into a pleasing shape and keep the tree as long as it would stand; its twisted limbs and scars marked more than a century of struggle for survival against all forces of nature. Like the ancient white pine beside the stone grill, the American Holly needed to be a memorial to its own longevity and to the families who preceded us on the farmstead.

Do not misunderstand, I liked a chain saw as well as the next guy. City folk want a reciprocating saw that will cut whenever cutting is difficult; open a room, remove a wall. In the mountains, I needed a chain saw, the longer the blade the better. Fell a dead oak for firewood; make quick work of deadfall. Still, when it came to living trees, I would cut when I must, but not before.

As I mentioned above, one of the natural threats to the flora is wind. We seemed to have a big wind at least every couple weeks, except in summer. To me, a "big" wind was a steady twenty-five to thirty miles per hour wind with gusts exceeding forty. One winter, gusts of more than sixty were reported in the cove, and a nearby friend reported that Flat Top Mountain (at the top of our cove) regularly experienced winds of eighty to one hundred miles per hour.

The cove was fairly narrow at our land, and we were at the head of the cove where the surrounding mountains rose above us. I expected that we would have some protection from big winds. Maybe we did; I could often hear a distant drone when standing in the pasture -- winds high up on the ridges that did not fall into the cove.

But when the winds picked up late in the

evening, our chimes began to sing. As the winds grew, there was a distinct crescendo of wind tumbling noisily down the forested ridge, a swelling roar that culminated in the vibration of the cabin walls and the rattling of the windows. It would wake you out of a sound sleep. It woke Beth one night when I was traveling.

No doubt it was the wind that woke her. But when she turned over to listen, she could tell that Nick, our black cat, was restless. She quickly turned on a light (remember the bat episode). Nick was staring at the ceiling. Beth looked, then heard the pitter patter of tiny flying squirrel feet and lots of them, a veritable expeditionary force trooping over the ceiling under the roof. Nick could not get them, nor could they get Beth. Nick was frustrated; Beth was pleased. The tramping continued despite Beth's attempts to scare them by tapping on the ceiling; I suppose the brilliant little rodents realized they were as safe from her as she from them.

Then she heard the BIG NOISE, a cracking, ripping, tearing sound. A large tree breaking nearby. She went out front and peered into the night but could not see a fallen walnut tree across the driveway or anything else unusual, so she went back in and tried to go back to sleep.

The next morning, she took Scout, our black lab, out for his morning constitutional. He had barely reached the bottom step when he stopped, assumed an attack crouch and barked. That was when Beth saw the garage, or what was left of the garage. A limb more than eighteen inches in diameter had fallen from the big maple beside the garage. The size of a healthy tree in its own right, the limb had completely demolished the garage.

Fortunately, the maple looked just fine even after losing a major limb. The garage needed some restorative work anyway; the breakage provided incentive. The main problem was going to be finding a contractor who was willing to restore the garage without insisting that it look newly constructed: there was much of the material that could be reused, if the contractor was willing. On second thought, I realized that the main problem was going to be getting a contractor willing to do the work at all.

HOMESCHOOLING

When Beth and I began to search for a new home, we looked in rural locations that did not always offer good school options. With her background in early childhood education, Beth decided she wanted to try homeschooling. She discovered that North Carolina has an active homeschooling community, especially in the mountains near Asheville, though much of that community sought independence from the public school system due to strict religious beliefs, such as creationism. That was not our motivation. We also learned that "homeschooling" is not limited to the home.

Beth joined a large, loose-knit group of homeschooling parents that, among other things, formed a one day a week private school so that they could collectively hire teachers for special subjects: for instance, an actor to teach Shakespeare, a physician mother to teach biology to middle-school students, a French woman to teach French. Area museums offered special homeschooling programs and often special rates. The parents were creative in searching for vital and productive ways for the children to learn.

Although homeschooling is a challenge for any parent who seriously accepts the responsibility, Beth has both the background (she specialized in Early Childhood Education in college, founded a day care center and taught in both public and private schools) and the motivation to find the resources to be sure that the children are learning and performing above their current grade levels. She savored being personally responsible for our children's education and being constantly involved in their learning, whether in or out of class. All in all, we found that because we had responsibility for their education, we were always looking for ways to encourage learning, much of it outside of the classroom.

The advantage of a small student to teacher ratio is amazingly powerful in the homeschool setting. Beth could teach more pages per day (not that she measured progress that way) than a public school teacher could ever accomplish with the large class populations. There were no distracting issues like cliques, fashion, drugs or sex. As for the issue of socialization, we found many homeschooled youth are more comfortable engaging in conversation with others, including adults (who frequently note the difference), than children taught in public school.

Where the public schools have been forced to abandon teaching music, art and physical education (unless you are selected for the school sports teams), our children had the time and resources to study the core courses and still devote energy to non-academic pursuits like horseback-riding or ballroom dance or pottery. With respect to sports, the county recreation department, especially soccer (both seasonal and indoor), offered plenty of options. The WNC Wildlife Center had summer volunteer positions that both our children joined as Junior Naturalists to answer visitor question about the animals, handle the snakes for demonstrations and prevent the guests from tormenting the goats. Any way we viewed their experiences, we were always pleased with having chosen to avoid some of the irrational incompetence of some public school administrations.

The shed was a fine school, allowing Beth and the children a space outside of the cabin to devote to scholastic work, a space they could leave an experiment set up without interfering with dinner. It also provided some of its own learning opportunities. Wrens nested inside as did the winter field mice. There was a map wall and snake skins hanging from the exposed rafters. Flash cards and books and supplies for writing or drawing or dissecting earthworms and frogs. There was small window above the desk that looked across the upper pasture toward the log barn. In a moment of reflection, Taylor witnessed a tawny bobcat traipse across the pasture from the woods to the creek, disappearing in a sudden leap.

When the school bus with its piercingly bright safety strobe broke the pre-dawn darkness whining up the road to pick up students from the cove, beeping in reverse to turn around at the end of the road, I was never sad that our children did not have to wait in the cold and dark to depart for school more than an hour before classes began.

In short, it worked for us, but it *was* work for Beth.

WORKING FROM HOME

I worked from the cabin, some days sitting for hours in front of the computer screen creating and amending spreadsheets for financial forecasts. My working world was narrative coupled with numbers, how markets translated into financial performance. I peered into a changing future daily; it was all voodoo. That does not mean it was not real, just that the reality was pending while we gazed into our crystal balls and hoped that events would unfold in a rational manner as we tried to make the future what we needed for it to be. Sometimes it was.

Most of my work remained in Atlanta. With five

telephone lines (the days before tablets and iPhones etc.), I maintained phone, fax and internet contact with the rest of the world. I leaned on the land lines for years as the cellular service was indifferent to my need to work.

When Beth and our children were in the cabin, I would usually talk outside on the cell phone. The reception along the creek was better anyway. If I forgot that I had picked up a wireless land line, the connection sputtered as I reached the pasture. If I was lucky, my caller would comment before I lost the connection. The worst place for a phone call was inside the cabin. Rain and winter weather presented some interesting logistics. Wanting to be beside the fire, but without a strong connection, I would venture onto the porch in boxers, fleece and unlaced hiking boots.

Our children developed a different view of my work habits. They noted that I would wander outside when I was going to yell at someone. I do not remember yelling much (except at the idiots at the phone company for inexplicable failures of service), but they saw me as "the phone king." I have known a few phone kings and know I fall short, but the humor was seeing myself through their eyes.

Talking on the phone or replying to emails put me anywhere on the planet that I wanted to be. No one I spoke with cared from where I was calling. Most assumed I was seated in an air-conditioned office with a water cooler, soft drink machine, bad coffee and a view of other office buildings and a parking lot. That was good for me so long as I did not cry out when I tripped over a boulder or suffered the fall of a large walnut onto my skull.

SELF-SUFFICIENCY

There were many pleasures of living at the cabin, almost all of which originated with a change in our view of the world and how we chose to live in it. There were dreams we had about how we could live our lives, what we would value and how our happiness would spring from what we did for ourselves and for others, what we could make, not take.

One element of this change was making things ourselves. As I wrote earlier, I am a mechanical idiot. I simply have no talent for inventing and constructing. But I do enjoy making things, whether rustic furniture, plumbing systems or food. The making of anything is made easier by the right tools and room to work. For projects that we chose to tackle, I made a point of having the right tools as much as feasible without purchasing one of everything that Home Depot or Lowe's sell, and there was plenty of room, either out of doors, in the garage, the shed (before we turned it into a school), or the barn.

My first big project (big for me though not for any of my woodworking friends) was a picnic table. I could not find any for sale. Thus, I knew I had to build it if we wanted to have a table for guests and not be limited to eating inside or seated in the chairs outdoors. Sounds easy, right? That was why I thought I could handle it.

The first step was to know what I wanted to build. How many would it seat, providing for gracious space shoulder to shoulder? How high off the ground would the benches be? It may seem obvious that you should begin at the beginning, but that was not always how I began. Having worked myself into an enthusiasm for a project, I was too often like the greyhound released on the race track: I was ready to run and chase without necessarily having evaluated whether I was interested in catching a rabbit.

Knowing what you want to build, where you want to end up, is the point of departure. And that was where it got complicated: long or short, high or low, room for six or twelve, attached benches or loose? Many more questions than a simple picnic table should require. But there it was. Decisions are an unavoidable way-station on the path to self-sufficiency.

I searched the internet for guidance and found some excellent freeware that enabled an erstwhile designer such as me to input certain criteria like lumber size and have the program spit out a design with all the pieces calculated and counted. I labored over the software for a couple of hours, playing with dimensions and capacity and aesthetics. Finally, I had a custom-designed table that would hold as many as twelve (eight comfortably). I bought the lumber (top and benches were eight-foot stock to reduce sawing) and nails and a new radial saw (another manly tool) and proceeded to build the table. Being the first project at the cabin and being the first time that we would be able to eat outside without feeling like we were camping out, Beth and the kids took great interest in my progress, even moaning with me when I smashed my thumb while nailing a cross-support to the underside of the table top.

In a few hours it was done. All told, it had taken less than six hours to design, provision and construct. My kind of "big" project. And we had a table, space for food and wine and utensils and lanterns and candles. A dining experience. Room for a feast.

We set the table in our new outdoor room. New in that now it had a piece of real furniture. Room in that it was bounded on the west side by a large black walnut tree and on the south side by the boxwood hedge. In the yard to the side of the cabin, but not visible from the road. Open, but private. Suitable for candlelight and lingering dinners with friends. Equally suitable for a lovely blue sky lunch when morning breezes still breathed softly and the summer heat had not yet smothered the cove.

****

For our first Christmas, Beth gave me something that I had wished for many times, but not yet taken the initiative to follow through. She gave me a brewing kit, ale pail and all. We were going to make our own beer. Or rather ale.

I read the book, reviewed the instructions, and solicited assistance from our daughter. Ten year old Taylor volunteered to be my number one Assistant Brewer and Chief Label Designer. I remembered my early days in college when I spent an interminable hour and half per week in a depressing basement chemistry lab. I remembered the chemistry lecture hall and how I stopped wasting my mornings there after the third or fourth visit. I remembered that, while I may have passed the chemistry exam, I had failed the lab and learned nothing that I can recall today except how to spell "titration".

Titration is not a core skill for humans. But brewing is essential chemistry. Water, barley, hops and yeast. Fermenting is the chemical reaction. A living substance, the yeast, consumes the sugars of the grain (barley). Water is the medium, hops the aroma and key to the flavor. I stared at the directions and felt the primal fear of a man beginning a precise titration. Tubes, siphon and bung. There were temperatures to be maintained, oxygen to be avoided, carbon dioxide to be released and a hygrometer to measure the resulting specific gravity. To quell my fear, I focused on the end result, the product. An ale made in my own pail and by my own hand.

The boiling wort smelled like sweet but rancid syrup, which malt is, sort of. Taylor and I stirred away for nearly an hour, washed by the steaming vapors. Then I hauled the hot brew to the creek, placed the pot into the swift cold stream for chilling and settling of the trub.

I do not know about you, but there is something ugly in even thinking about drinking something called "wort" that produces "trub". But there we were. A cold winter's day, balancing on a rock in the creek trying not to step into the creek or spill the hot wort, no doubt an environmental offense reportable to the EPA and requiring disclosure to subsequent purchasers of the land. A downstream cataclysm for aquatic creatures.

Despite my killing the yeast by dumping the small bag into the too-hot wort as soon as I turned off the propane, the ale survived. We loved it. We called our production Bad Dog Brewery.

We made a simple amber ale first. Magnificent! We called it Hare o' the Dog since we could not decide whether to name it for the rabbits in the pasture or our namesake brewery dog. It was a dark and nutty ale with substance enough for a winter night. Then we brewed another batch to try to avoid some of the mistakes of the first batch and then on to a pale ale or three.

The first pale ale was tasty, light with pleasant hops (Summertime Brew). The next pale ale (Summertime Brew ESP) was a slightly more involved recipe that called for me to steep a bag of barley before I boiled the malt. The result was darker than the first, full-bodied and flavorful, but more bitter than I prefer. The last ale (Almost Autumn Amber or Bad Dog Brown) was a perfect balance of hops, but still a bit darker than I desired for a summer ale. Once summer passed into fall, we returned to the original amber recipe with a finer liquid yeast.

The results were beyond our expectations. My family rewarded me on Father's Day with an embroidered cap bearing Bad Dog Brewery and the head of a Labrador. Although we made it purely for family and friends, it felt like the brewery had become real once I had a hat to prove it.

In mid-September, we went to the annual Great Smokies Craft Brewers' Festival in downtown Asheville. Brewgrass, as it is called for short, is a classic Asheville festival blending the best of a college street party (unlimited sampling of good beers and ales in a totally casual, body-pierced, tattoo-adorned, outdoor gear atmosphere) along with honest-to-goodness bluegrass music, the sound of these mountains, a music that is purely American but organically Celtic. My roots exactly. More than three dozen microbreweries attended and offered their best for sampling. I wore my hat, hoping that someone would notice and inquire; not a soul asked where they could taste the best of Bad Dog Brewery. On the other hand, we drank only one or two beers that I thought tasted better than what we crafted at the cabin, the credit for which goes to our well water and Andy's expert guidance. Andy owned Asheville Brewery Supply, on Wall Street at the time, and provided the ingredients and instructions.

The next big project that we tackled as a family was the garden. Once again, we knew little about what we wanted in the way of a garden, though we had plenty of ideas about what we wanted *in* the garden. The kids wanted pumpkins and watermelons. Beth wanted all the usual—tomatoes, peppers, squash, zucchini, string beans—plus broccoli, brussel sprouts, beets and carrots. Cantaloupe. Onions and arugula. Corn, as much for the stalks (autumn decoration) as the ears. All of it sounded delicious to me except for the beets.

So how much space did we need? Or want to cultivate? Beth studied and researched and questioned friends who had had large gardens in the past. We managed to postpone planting by procrastination until after a surprisingly late frost the second week of May, when many friends lost their newly planted tomato plants.

I dutifully acquired a tiller, another manly tool in my burgeoning arsenal. Unlike Beth, I had been able to find no one who could give me practical guidance about the size tiller we would need. So, as usual, I winged it. We did not know how hard it might be to break the ground for a garden; it had been more than a decade (maybe five) since anyone had worked this land, and we knew (remembering the trenching for the underground power line) there could be loads of rocks to be churned up and removed. I read that a front tine tiller was good for a small corner-of-the-yard kind of garden. Anything larger and I needed a rear tine tiller. I researched "tine" to understand what they meant (I never fully comprehended the term, but I came to believe it referred to the tilling blades). Then I settled on a seven horsepower rear tine tiller with self-powered wheels and a reverse gear. I had visions of plowing dawn to dusk over a three day weekend to be able to till the ground to an acceptable consistency. The machine would not even fit into the back of the Land Cruiser until they removed the packing materials at the hardware store. And I still had to put it together, requiring almost as many tools as the total in my possession; in fact, I was a crescent wrench or two short and had to improvise. It quickly looked like I had bitten off more than I needed much less could handle.

Tilling nearly tore my back from my frame, practically removed my arms from their shoulder sockets. There were places where the tiller jumped and heaved and sped away from me as if pulled by a demon draft horse or a manic mule with no conscience. I could barely hang on. So I reread the owner's manual. It recommended a gentle hand. I remarked on the jerking and leaping it had done and thought there was a conspiracy to eliminate weak gardeners like me. Surely a gentle hand would empower the machine to take complete control and till me under with the grass and weeds. Nevertheless, yielding to those more knowledgeable than me, I tried. In some ways, it worked. The trick was to lift the handle slightly to prevent the tines biting deeply into the soil and outrunning the slower self-powered wheels. Instead of snatching my back out of my frame, the tiller simply pulled my muscles to the limits of elasticity. Pained, but not broken.

All in all, it went better than it might have. In some ways, it went better than I expected. At the end of my first hour, we had a space 30 feet by 60 feet that had been tilled to a depth of several inches (not consistently but on average). There were a few rocks to remove and heaps of weeds and grass tilled rootless.

I wanted to take all the credit but the soil seemed to have been cultivated before. Maybe it was just a barnyard effect, the tramping of a hundred hooves, the waste of dozens of cattle. A herd repeated over time. I could not be sure. But it smelled right to me. Rich, loamy, manure-cured dirt. The kind of soil that *should* produce a crop.

Beth and our children had planned the layout of the garden with nice pathways giving access to six planting areas. They had planned which plants would go in each area: pumpkins, gourds, watermelons and cantaloupe in one area, carrots, beets, beans and brussel sprouts in another. All the squash and zucchini clustered together and bounded by peppers and cucumbers. They marked the pathways with oak stakes salvaged from the tractor barn.

Cameron (then six) worried about the benches we would need along the paths; I asked why and he said that we needed a place for our "customers" to rest. We had not discussed having a commercial operation so we were not quite sure where he conjured that notion.

Of course, nothing is as easy as it looks on paper. With the soil tilled and the crops decided, we had only to plant and let nature take its course. Maybe, sort of, but not really.

We laid a heavy layer of mulch down the pathways, then began to plant. The children took the lead; I traipsed off to mow the pastures. A few hours later, when I returned to check their progress, they had nearly completed the planting. And the rows were, how should I say, not entirely plumb line straight. But each row was planted with seeds of the same kind and each row had a generous separation from its neighboring row, so we seemed to have implemented a plan that would result in a garden. Again, maybe.

Everyone reveled in their contribution to the effort, and everyone had truly contributed. We fussed a bit over lingering weeds, laid more mulch, said our prayers and left it all alone. Sun and rain, sun and rain.

All we needed was sun and rain. Germinate the seeds and ignite the growth. Wait and watch for the unfolding of small seedlings into tiny leaves pushing inexorably upward through rough ground while simultaneously thrusting incipient roots downward in search of nutrients and moisture. Tiny, fragile, sparks of life springing from the dry buried seeds of our hopes.

Our first garden summer was hotter than our first summer at the cabin. Temperatures consistently reached into the eighties. Rain was sparse, mostly from scattered summer thunderstorms, the kind that are so scattered that they can miss you for days in a row while the next mountain over is having small floods. At first, we would supplement the rain with watering. Later, as summer waned and the creek waned with it, we realized that rain was nowhere to be found. Dry clear days, perfect for anything except growing crops.

I finally decided there was no reason to hope for the beans, and I plowed them under. The lettuce had gotten out of control, too large and bitter, so I plowed it. The collards, broccoli and brussel sprouts never really grew more than about eight inches, so I also plowed them under. The corn had grown all the ears it could grow, so we cut it down and dried the stalks for Halloween. The zucchini braved the heat and drought, continually surprising us with the forever-overlooked Monster Zuke. Only the jalapenos seemed energized by the hot dry August; but I guess that made sense, didn't it?

Beth and I considered whether we should water the garden. Some neighbors were watering; others not. Some neighbors were losing water pressure, if only temporarily. Warren, a friend who lived behind us up near the top of the ridge, called a well company and they told him how lucky he was that his loss of water had been temporary; most of the calls they were getting came from people who had lost their wells completely. We agreed that the creek was mighty low and, since we did not know how deep our well extended, we might be asking for trouble if we used the well to water. (Later we learned that our well was about one hundred five feet deep with a flow of ten gallons per minute, plenty for our family. On the other hand, Warren's was over four hundred twenty-five feet deep (his house was about three hundred feet above our cabin) and flowed only one gallon per minute. His well pipe was his reservoir.)

The dry hot summer gave us insight into the difficult lives of subsistence farmers who preceded us. What if we depended on the garden for our food? What if we depended on what we grew to feed the family through the winter until the next year's harvest? What if we depended on the garden for a surplus that we could sell or trade for other goods or services that we needed? A bushel of tomatoes for the doctor, hardware store or haberdasher? What if. We would have an entirely serious and anxious appreciation for weather and especially rain, which needed to be sufficient, but not in excess.

Prayers and skywatching may help or not. We

did both anyway. We wanted rain more than we needed it, but we felt the loss of a diminishing creek flow -- the bold and noisy creek had thinned to a whispering trickle -- dying plants and unproductive walnut trees.

For all this land must have seen over the previous one hundred fifty years, surely it had survived similar periods of drought. If the trees and creek survived before, it would survive again. So we thought. Then we learned that our drought might become the longest, most severe drought in the recorded history of North Carolina. And, of course, the demands on natural resources today were greater than during earlier centuries. Back then, when first settled, the cove would have supported only a couple of families and a herd of cattle roaming the woods and ridges during the summer. In modern times, every one of seventy or more families was pulling water from the earth every day. If, like other water tables across the country, our local water table was declining, the impact would be felt in wells but also in the survivability of trees.

We could dwell on the possibility of the worst, but considered it better to acknowledge what could happen and then improve what we could.

Ultimately, it took a wandering tropical storm sliding northward from the Gulf of Mexico to bring the first real rain in over a month. By that time the garden was mostly gone, leaving several watermelons stunted mid-growth and all the pumpkin vines dried like thick twine. The tomatoes had grown smaller and smaller until the usually robust Better Boys looked more like inflated cherry tomatoes.

Nevertheless, we had enjoyed learning the ways and manners of our garden. We had consumed more than our share of our own produce with plenty to give to friends, a triumph in itself. Tomatoes so juicy and tasty that you would swear they had been salted. Zucchini galore that Beth converted into magnificent and exotic soups. Tender, savory salad greens. A few bell peppers, jalapenos, crook necked squash and tiny malformed carrots. Big bulbous beets that I did not eat, but Beth loved. We harvested a couple of rather small pumpkins and a few gourds; despite some disappointment that we did not have a single county fair competitor, we relished the satisfaction of having grown anything at all.

We could not wait until we could try again.

The bane of our gardening was moles. After the reasonable success of our first year, especially given the challenges of the drought, our subsequent years were plagued – literally – by moles. Vicious, tunnel-digging, root-killing moles.

Moles survive by eating Japanese beetle larvae. Grubs. Fat, juicy white nuggets of worm (yes, I know larva is not technically a worm). Scoop a handful of soil from our garden and uncover several healthy grubs.

I researched mole control and learned that "mole control" is an oxymoron. There seemed to be plenty of theories, but nothing that truly succeeded.

From the purveyors of fine, back-to-the-earth,

non-electric products, Lehman's, I purchased a mole windmill. It was a small galvanized windmill that is designed to set atop a steel pipe (not included) that you drive into the ground. The theory is that the winds blow, the windmill turns atop the pipe, and the clicking and clacking reverberates through the soil, causing the moles to seek quieter pastures. Literally.

Nope. Sounded good, but a month and more after installation there were massive tunnel ridges running all across the garden and around the windmill pole. Quite likely it was sound technology (sic) and I just had unfavorable conditions like the wrong kind of soil. But then the right kind of soil probably would not grow any produce.

I continued searching without any success for something that worked, something to chase away the moles if not the blues. But, thank goodness we were not dependent on our productivity to survive the winter. And thank goodness the mole windmill did not cost as much as some of our big tools. In the end, I did like seeing it spin as I stood in the bathroom looking across the upper pasture to the barn, the shiny blades tracing empty and useless circles in the air.

PAIN AND SUFFERING

Living in the country exacts a certain payment in blood, sweat and tears. With the pleasant summer temperatures, we had relatively little of the sweat, but plenty of the blood and tears.

Scratched by the occasional wayward strand of barbwire. Splinters from firewood and salvage lumber. Slamming my thumb with a 20 oz. hammer while constructing the picnic table. Singed hair and small third degree burns from sticking my hands into the woodstove to place a fresh log on the white hot embers. Too many nicked knuckles and shins to mention. And, of course, here and there, a blister or two.

Now, I did not want to sound like I was complaining because I knew that outdoor life is nothing if not an opportunity to shed a bit of skin.

Cameron was the only family member to have attracted the actual sting of a stinging insect. Neither time was he doing anything that you might expect of a boy; in other words, he was not poking a stick in a wasps' nest or shaking a tree with a hornets' nest dangling from the limb.

Nope, once he was just running across the upper pasture when an overly affectionate stinging something nailed him. He cried a bit, but shook it off and returned to the field. The second time he was stung, he was sitting under the shed at the side of the barn when an insect zipped out of nowhere, nailed him on the back of his head and disappeared. All four of us had been sitting in the shade talking, but the nasty creature hit Cameron only. It was another week before I discovered what had become a modestly large hornets' nest under the shed. It had not been noticeable at the time Cameron got stung.

Cameron had a few days with multiple scrapes, but mostly it was just kid stuff. Same with Taylor.

We saw the first Harry Potter movie the day of its release. Taylor and I had read the books; Beth and Cameron loved the movie. Cameron returned to the cabin determined to anoint himself with a lightning scar across his forehead just like Harry's. Fortunately, he used a crayon and acquiesced when we tried to convince him that earning a real scar would probably come in time, but at a price.

We were also blessed that neither Taylor nor Cameron had any serious mishaps. It would have been so easy to fall from the barn loft, trip on a creek rock, surprise a snake in the woods or simply stick a finger where a spider already was. Cameron claimed to slip and fall in the creek with some frequency, but then he seemed mighty pleased to be soaking wet in the summertime.

All in all, both of our children adapted to the watchfulness necessary to living more out of doors than in. Then again, I never tempted fate by turning them loose with heavy equipment.

Briars are living things. Yes, living because they are plants, but that is not what I mean. They are living creatures, like animals. More particularly, like a spider or an octopus or some other multi-legged creature.

The land was plagued with briars when we arrived. Years of neglect created the ideal growth environment. Harry, my landscape architect friend, said that briars are early stage recovery flora. I think he meant that, after everything vegetative has been eliminated from a place, whether by natural (fire) or unnatural (pesticide or clear-cutting) causes, the briar is one of the first plants to stake a claim on recovery. For that reason, the briar thrives in the stark sunlight of newly denuded pastureland and withers to near-extinction in the shade of maturing woodlands.

Anyway, we had more briars than we wanted and did not appreciate the niche the briar fills in the ecological pantheon. I wanted to be able to get into the woods or down to the creek bank without risk of bleeding to death from thorn punctures and lacerations. I began to cut away. First with the not so faithful weedeater, then with a machete from Haiti, some ritualistic blade intended no doubt for voodoo ceremony in the islands. I very ceremoniously dismembered every briar thicket I could reach.

In doing so, I found that the briars reached out for me as if alive and vindictive, as if thoughtful in the way any carnivorous plant can appear to be, the tendrils of thorn reached out and stuck and gouged and snagged and ripped me.

Armed with briar-proof hunting pants, a thick shirt, hat and gloves, I marched into the fray. Carefully, with thoughtful movement and strategy, I aimed the blade for the base of the thicket; then I swung. An eviscerating chop to the trunk of the briar, a fresh pale green wound where I severed trunk from root. Of course, during the attack, I kept low to the ground, eyes scrunched and shoulders hunched against the potential backlash.

Success! I would step away from the thicket and admire my martial prowess. The felled thicket with trunks of varying ages and dimensions, from the freshest green of yearling shoots to the rough and gnarly brown bark of thick-trunked survivors.

On to the next, I would say, then stride away to the next downstream thicket, slashing small stragglers along the way, turning to admire my progress as I advanced.

Thus a short winter afternoon would pass as I worked along the edges of the pasture and creek bank, clearing all I could clear. Swinging and chopping and slashing; all the while ducking and slouching and, occasionally, gingerly removing stubborn thorns like dragon teeth buried in my skin.

Finally, content with my efforts for the day, the enemy beaten if not vanquished, I strode homeward to hearth and kin, "home is the hunter" as it were. I returned to the cabin, smiling as the victor victorious and satisfied with my accomplishment, until Beth remarked upon my bloody chin and eyebrows, streaks of dried blood lining my cheeks, and declared me the victim.

It was not all work around the cabin. When I ventured across the pasture on my way to the compost heap or the woodside briar thickets, I usually passed a ball or ten, remnants of our attempts to teach our Labrador retriever to retrieve (something I thought was genetic). Never having lost my love of soccer, I cannot pass a ball on the ground without kicking it. A while back, I had been slashing through a thicket at the north end of the pasture and was returning toward the cabin when I approached the soccer ball resting quietly in the grass. So I kicked it. Not out of any malice mind you; it just seemed the thing to do, a soccer ball in my path waiting to do what soccer balls do, leap from the end of a foot.

I gave no thought to the chain saw dangling from my right hand, blade safely (so I thought) pointed behind me. As I cocked my leg for the kick, I pulled my right foot back and up as hard and as quickly as I could. That part worked nicely; I connected my ankle bone with the bar of the chain saw just so. Bone on blade, a perfect connection resulting in extreme pain.

But then I followed through and kicked the bejeebers out of the soccer ball and kept walking. My ankle hurt, but it was a good swift kick, so I felt some redemption. Besides, there were more briars and brush to cut along the creek.

Thursday night was game night at the cabin. Kids' choice. We gathered at the kitchen table so that Taylor and Cameron could slaughter me and Beth at any of a variety of games: Blisters (a dice game based on hiking the Appalachian Trail), Parcheesi, Monopoly, whatever. On the Thursday following the Sunday soccer kick, we had finished our game of Parcheesi when the kids decided they needed to jump on my back a few times before going to bed. We horsed around a bit beside the wood stove, then they went to their room.

Later I commented to Beth that I must have pulled something; my ankle ached.

It hurt badly again the next day, so I hobbled a bit. A few days later, I could not walk and could not get comfortable even lying still on the sofa. You bet, I had broken my ankle. I am a lousy patient and refused to have a cast, choosing instead to nurse the break it with a "boot" cast and ace wraps.

In the meantime, I could see the briars smiling. I was, for a while, out of action.

In late October, we invited a few friends for a bonfire and dinner. Michael, a close friend from Atlanta came up early with his dogs to help prepare. We ran some errands, drove to the top of the cove and briefly explored an old farmstead that lies across the top of a ridge, then returned to the cabin to lay a fire in the stone grill and set the bonfire in the lower pasture.

About an hour before people were to begin arriving, Les (remember the wood guy?) called to say that he had my firewood on his truck and would be delivering it shortly. Which he did. He used an old chipper truck for delivery and simply pulled a lever to elevate the rear and spill the firewood on the ground. Which he did.

There was a jumbled pile of firewood in front of the neatly stacked cord that I had previously bought from Harlan Sawyer (no kidding, a sawyer named Sawyer).

Michael, ever energetic, declared that he was going to stack the newly delivered load. I discouraged him as guests would be arriving soon, and I did not want people thinking that I had invited them to work before they ate. But Michael insisted. He wanted an "outdoor" experience. It was an overcast cold autumn day that quickly turned to snow showers as we began to stack the wood.

If he was going to stack our firewood, then I felt obliged to stack also.

He wanted each of us to walk from the pile to the stack, but I insisted that he toss me the wood from the pile so that I could stack more quickly.

"It'll go faster if you just toss the logs to me and I'll stack them," I suggested.

"I think that's a bad idea," responded Michael.

"If we're going to do this, I want to finish before people start arriving, so just toss them to me," I persisted.

Michael began picking logs from the pile and tossing to me to stack into a neat cord. We should have realized that it was an idea that might not work with complete success when, after several good tosses, a short toss by Michael resulted in a log landing on my foot. It did not hurt, but I gave him a scowl that remonstrated caution.

He smiled and assured me he would be more careful, at the same time reminding me that he thought playing catch was a bad idea.

A few logs later, as I was looking downward to place another log on the stack, a severe pain exploded at the top of my head. Hit by a log!

I immediately raised my hand to my head and felt for blood. Nothing.

Michael came over to me. "Let me see."

I lowered my head and he examined the site.

"Looks okay. A little skinned but nothing bad."

"Good. Hurts like hell, but I guess I can continue."

I removed my hand from pressure on my head to begin stacking again, and a warm course of blood rushed over my forehead and down my nose.

Michael looked across the pile and said, "Well, maybe it's worse than I thought. You better get Beth to look at it."

I toddled back toward the cabin, soaking my glove as I walked. Beth looked at my injury and did not think that I needed to get stitches. Not needing stitches, I did not see any reason to go to the emergency room. I pressed a cold towel to the wound and held it tightly, trying to stop the bleeding. I asked Beth to prepare a bag of ice, so that I could treat the swelling as soon as I had the bleeding under control. I went back out to the wood pile to encourage Michael to give it up, but he would not.

As I stood talking with him, no longer pretending that I would assist since one hand was firmly pressed to my scalp, we chatted and tried to laugh. He observed how much worse it would have been if I had looked up at the moment of impact and taken the log in the eye, nose or mouth. He felt guilty, even though it was not his fault. I felt like the Black Knight in Monty Python's Holy Grail, who said, "It's only a flesh wound" while he bled arterially from severed limbs.

I stopped the bleeding before anyone arrived. I am tall enough that no one could see the oozing wound as we enjoyed the fires and low country boil in the cold dark of an early winter night. A few beers and a few painkillers, and I felt perfectly chipper.

CELEBRATING

Holidays, especially the big three of Halloween, Thanksgiving and Christmas, were rustically romantic at the cabin. When autumn colors descended the surrounding ridges, we piled hay bales at the ends of the split rail fence along our bridge over Trantham Creek. Beth braced tall bundles of dried corn stalks beside the spindly black walnuts that framed the driveway, tying them with seasonal rust and gold ribbon. The children stacked pumpkins on the hay bales, and we carved crazy jack o' lanterns with big ears to light on the porch. The cold holiday season began.

With frost sparkling across the wilted grass of the pastures and a sturdy plume of smoke rising from the stone chimney, fall clipped toward winter with fewer and fewer leaves rattling on bare limbs. The fresh chill in the air, a comforting fire in the family room, short days and a stack of firewood in the steel ring by the window on the front porch.

Halloween seemed to disappear too swiftly into Thanksgiving each year. One brief night of wandering through Norwood Park, an intown Asheville neighborhood whose denizens generously tolerated the outsiders trick or treating while the neighbors applauded costumes and drank wine on their porches. By the time the candy had been consumed, it was time to head north to our fishing cabin that we shared with friends.

The fishing cabin was more remote and wild than Mole Ranch. Four of us rented the cabin on a prominent trout stream in the mountains of western Virginia. The other three fishing friends munificently allowed our family to have the cabin for the week of Thanksgiving. Often it was the only week-long vacation we had as a family. We always smoked a turkey breast after spending most of the week standing in the cold river waving a fly rod and hoping to attract wily rainbows and browns. Sometimes we lucked into snow and mornings icy enough to light the tiny woodstove that soon forced us to open a window and let the outside in despite burning only an armful of small twigs.

When we returned from Virginia, we leapt into Christmas preparations and decorations. The outside essentials included a large wreath of Virginia creeper, a kind of wild grape that climbs tall trees with its own thick trunk and curling tendrils that wrap around small branches, which we hung on the tractor barn wall facing the downstream bend of the road below the lower pasture. A spotlight lit the wreath with its big red bow against the vertical board and batten of the barn. Another spotlight lit a smaller traditional wreath on the wide door to the shed, left of the cabin. To the right and back of the rear porch, two spots lit twin wreaths on each of the hill house doors. Lastly, the lights of the

Christmas tree twinkled through the front window of the cabin flanked by candles in the windows. Admittedly, we were proud of the Christmas lights and hoped that our neighbors living up the mountain enjoyed seeing the cabin festive for the season.

One afternoon before our third Christmas, an SUV pulled to the side of the road and stopped just past our mailbox. Wondering if they were having car trouble, I headed down the driveway. As I approached our bridge, I called to the man who had opened the rear hatch door, "Need help?"

He was stretching into the cargo area, but paused to signal that he was okay. As I continued toward the road, he closed the door and walked toward me.

"We really appreciate what you have done with the place and love the Christmas lights." He handed me a music CD titled Celtic Christmas. We later learned that Al is a well-known Grammy winner who, along with his wife Amy, makes the rounds playing traditional acoustic music. We had no idea that they lived on the mountain up the watershed from us.

We started our cabin Christmas traditions the first year with an open house for friends and neighbors. On the evening of our first open house, we feared we had failed. The initial time for the open house came and went. Not a soul arrived. An hour later, no one had come and no one had called to say they were not coming (we had not requested RSVP). Beth and I mumbled to each other incredulous inanities as we searched for an explanation. Wrong date on the invitations? Wrong time? Wrong address? Nope, no, not. We were still too new to the area to know a neighbor we were comfortable calling.

Food was spread across the breakfast table and the picnic table. Bowls of punch chilled beside stacks of paper cups. Thermoses of warm apple cider and coffee stood resting on the kitchen counter. Happy fires burned in the woodstove and outside in the stone grill.

What was happening?

Not five minutes past one hour later than the starting time of the open house, after the last glow of sunset had vanished over the ridge, swallowed by the dark of an early night, we peered out the windows one last desperate time and spied a literal parade of car lights turning onto the bridge and winding between the shed and tractor barn into the "parking lot" of the upper pasture.

Relief. Friends and more friends. New friends and their families. At one point during the night we tallied forty-two people inside the tiny cabin, twenty-four of whom were children. The joy of that celebration was matched over the years only by other cabin Christmases.

Every year was different even though many of the guests were the same. One warm year when the children were older, they dashed madly around in the dark, scaring each other in the barn and woods, but unafraid of the night. Cold years we clustered around the blaze in the stone grill. One night it snowed so heavily that we knew people might not be able to make it safely; we considered postponing. But friends arrived anyway, though all but one couple were from our side of the mountain. Joe, the carpenter who reconstructed the tractor barn following the maple tree mishap, and his wife Lisa were the only friends to make it all the way out from town, but then Lisa is an Alaskan. It was another special night.

Each of the holidays in the cabin was unique in its way. The constant was the warmth of friends around the fire, the celebratory lights, the rustic comfort and embrace of a holiday gathering. All were a time for love and peace. And the last open house lasted the longest as people said their farewells to the cabin and finished the remaining bottles of Bad Dog Brewery ale: Bad Dog Brown, Autumn Amber and Scout Stout.

EPILOGUE

For five years we lived in our log cabin on the south side of the Swannanoa Mountains. We were happy to be there and never more happy than on September 11, 2001. When the shock of the destruction spread across our country that morning and the skies were silenced, we were relieved to be secure in a quiet cove a long way from big cities, our children free to run around our pasture and woods without fear of terrorist bombs.

I had been in Atlanta that morning. I called a friend as I left a breakfast meeting, and she told me that a plane had crashed into the World Trade Center. I asked her if there was bad weather in New York. When she replied No, I felt my heart drop, without really knowing why.

I immediately returned to my apartment and got on the computer. The internet was too jammed to be able to log onto any news source quickly, so I knew that something horrible must have happened. I turned to old-fashioned radio. The reporter on NPR was saying something about a plane crashing into the Pentagon. I thought it must be a modern version of Orson Wells' "War of the Worlds" broadcast. It was impossible for me to conceive that there had been two planes crashed – one in New York City and the other in Washington, D.C. -- with such impact in a single morning.

Without a clear understanding of what was going on, I knew that there was a potential for panic as workers in Atlanta left work early to return home. I knew I needed to be with my family and should leave quickly to be sure that I could get home.

It was after lunch when I arrived back at the

cabin and saw the first television coverage of what had happened. Relief is inadequate to express how good it felt to be home with my family.

We did not move to the mountains to escape anything. But we were happy to be in a place where it was more convenient than in some other places to be as self-sufficient as we wanted to be. We were pleased to be surrounded by people, many of whom we did not know initially, who were likewise happy to be free to depend upon themselves and their neighbors in a way that is often difficult in modern cities.

We settled into a lifestyle that was in no way reminiscent of the back-to-the-earth movement of the 1960s. But, we witnessed the changes in our planet and in the mountains. We felt the irreversible effects of weak environmental policy and unsustainable agricultural and fishery practices. We supported the local mountain pioneers who accepted the uncertainty and economic challenges of growing organic crops. We supported landowners who began to see that preservation of open land is essential to maintaining the mountains with which we all fell in love.

Even today, years after our departure, I can see all of the cabin property in plain detail, like a literary passage learned and memorized or an image of a favorite place. I know where the hidden flowers bloom -- trout lily, jack-in-the-pulpit, lady slipper – as well as where the giant hemlocks rise far into the canopy near the patches of ground juniper and just below the laurel "hell". I can see trout hovering invisible above pale shadows in their pools of sun, the crawdad rocks, the sandy creek bed and the lip of the creek bank where the bloodwort suddenly appears for the few days it blossoms each year. All of the memories bring me peace.

The mountains are changing. That is unavoidable. Nevertheless, we believe they can change while remaining the place of beauty and refuge they have so long been.

ABOUT THE AUTHOR

J. Privette grew up in eastern North Carolina and returned to the coast after living in the mountain cabin. He, Beth, Cameron and Scout live on a sailboat in the sailing town of Oriental. Taylor lives near her grandmother and aunt in Greensboro. They visit friends in the mountains when they can.